The B-26 Goes to War

Army's Torpedo Challenge

A Band of B-26 Pilots Join the Navy – Temporarily

5th Air Force – 22nd Bomb Group – South Seas Saga

Diary & Commentary by:

1st Lt. Frank S. Allen, Jr. (Col. USAF Retired)
1st Lt. Merrill Thomas Dewan (Lt. Col. USAF Reserve)
1st Lt. James P. Muri (Lt. Col. USAF Retired)

EDITED by
Jeanne Allen Newell
Tom Dewan
Joshua Muri
Brian Gibbons

Editor-in-Chief
Stan Walsh

authorHOUSE®

AuthorHouse™
1663 Liberty Drive
Bloomington, IN 47403
www.authorhouse.com
Phone: 1 (800) 839-8640

Published by AuthorHouse 02/14/2018

ISBN: 978-1-5462-2166-1 (sc)
ISBN: 978-1-5462-2165-4 (e)

Library of Congress Control Number: 2017919297

Print information available on the last page.

Any people depicted in stock imagery provided by Thinkstock are models,
and such images are being used for illustrative purposes only.
Certain stock imagery © Thinkstock.

This book is printed on acid-free paper.

Because of the dynamic nature of the Internet, any web addresses or links contained in
this book may have changed since publication and may no longer be valid. The views
expressed in this work are solely those of the author and do not necessarily reflect the
views of the publisher, and the publisher hereby disclaims any responsibility for them.

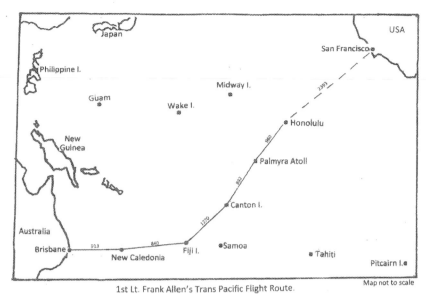

1st Lt. Frank Allen's Trans Pacific Flight Route.

Map not to scale

Mere Dots in Pacific Assume Importance as Stop-over Bases.

Distances in Miles:

Townsville to Reid River	35
" " Iron Range	498
" " Cape York	656
" " Cooktown	280
" " Port Moresby	679
" " Brisbane	692
" " Sydney	1318
Brisbane Sydney	570
Sydney Melbourne	540
Sydney Newcastle	35
Brisbane Perth	2241
Port Moresby Iron Range	328
" " Rabaul	500
" " Cooktown	434
" " Lae	188
" " Timor	1475
Darwin Brisbane	1831

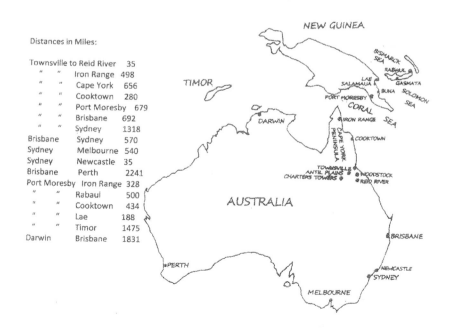

NOT TO SCALE

Contents

Dedication

Lest we forget . . . This book is dedicated to the men and women who conceived and crafted a flying machine worthy of earthly honors and to the airmen who followed their spirit to achieve everlasting praise for a mission well done.

Acknowledgements

We are tremendously indebted to Jeanne Allen Newell daughter, of Col. Frank Allen, for bringing to our attention and sharing her dad's unabridged commentary about his early B-26, 22nd BG flight experiences and the challenges he faced while developing a new unique weapons system. His keen observations recorded in a fresh narrative style inspired the creation of this book. Like the torpedo carrying fantasy, this book is also rashly experimental blending Allen's writings with the extraordinary combat diary entries by 1st Lt. Merrill Dewan, which were graciously made available by his Son, Thomas Dewan. To assure continuity, we further researched the comprehensive history of the 22nd BG, **Revenge of the Red Raiders** compiled by Lawrence J. Hickey. We thank Andrew W. Boehly, Marauder Archivist, Pima Air & Space Museum in Tucson AZ, for opening the 22nd BG file and providing rare photographs.

We offer many thanks to many people for sharing their knowledge and their support including: Marshall Magruder, President of the B-26 Marauder Historical Society (MHS), whose dynamic research abilities turns myths into clear historic truths; the MHS Staff, Phillip Gutt, Executive Director, Jennifer Merritt, Secretary; MHS Members including: Roberta Dow Faulkenberry, innovative reunion researcher-organizer; Bill Spurrier, instrumental in the digital preservation of nitrate film showing torpedo drop tests; Brian Gibbons for his tireless quest for Marauder facts and being the MHS Principal Marauder archivist; aviation artist Jack Fellows, for his dramatic cover art; Vernon Pack, literary reviewer and eagle-eye proof-reader; Peter and

Marcie Walsh and Keira Walsh-Wilson's family, for enthusiastic curiosity, encouragement and computer guidance; Steve and Barbara Swartz, unlimited MHS photographic coverage; Rosetta and Robin Williams, composition advisors plus their interest in all-things Marauder. We are also inspired by the Marauder *esprit de corps* exhibited by folks at, MAPS (Military Aviation Preservation Society), North Canton, OH; B-26 Archives, University of Akron, OH; Glenn L. Martin Maryland Aviation Museum, Middle River, Maryland; and by scholars and fans of military aviation history the world over. We thank you.

Preface

Here is the untold story of a youthful band of fly-boys in their brand new state-of-the-art flying machine, the Martin B-26 Marauder, flying "hell bent" without hesitation stopping cold the Japanese juggernaut descending on the Southwest Pacific. With fellow warriors on land and sea, they turned the tide in the Pacific. Their swift rugged airplane captivated the imagination of war-planners, who asked, "Why not have this short-wing wonder carry long-nose Navy torpedoes?" They were serious. So wheels turned and an order to make it happen was handed down. At grass-roots level no one was prepared for this directive but Yankee ingenuity kicked in and with passionate persistence an unlikely weapons system was born. The B-26 chalked-up the greatest combat record of all time but a glaring omission in its history is the true story of airmen attempting to turn this Army land-based bomber into an over-the-waves Navy torpedo carrier. Their exploits were intense, vivid and sometimes entertaining. We correct this over-sight and add a bit more luster to the memory of a premiere bombing group, its planes and its people who with determination, against all odds, sustained America's fighting strength during the chaotic first nine months of World War Two in the Pacific.

The arrival of the 22nd Bombardment Group in Australia in mid-March 1942 marked America's earliest organized response to Japan's aggressive advance in the Southwest Pacific. New airfields in the vicinity of Townsville on Australia's Coral Sea coast put Allied bombers within striking distance of the enemy. Thus began the battering of Japanese airfields and troop concentrations to prevent the fall of Port Moresby in Papua, New Guinea; they also enabled raids on Rabaul, the Japanese stronghold on New Britain Island.

New Guinea was the key objective of Japan's advance. The island as a whole dominates the waters in several directions – the open Pacific to the north, the Coral Sea to the southeast and the Solomon Sea to the east. At its closest point New Guinea is less than one hundred miles from the Australian mainland. The island, with the exception of the southern quarter known as the Territory of Papua, was destined to be in enemy hands. If the Japanese occupied the entire island they would dominate vital targets in northern Australia. Fortunately the southern coast of Papua remained in friendly hands.

The assault on New Guinea began 21 January 1942 when Japanese aircraft bombed Australian-controlled areas including Rabaul, seat of government for the Territory of New Guinea located on New Britain Island in the nearby Bismarck Archipelago. It fell 2 days later on 23 January 1942. The area was immediately turned into a formidable air and naval base. Other islands were occupied including New Ireland, the Admiralty Islands and Bougainville. Geographically these are part of the northern Solomon Islands. Taken together, these actions by the Japanese posed a very real threat to northern Australia – a threat underscored by the air attack on Darwin, capital of Australia's Northern Territory on 19 February 1942.

With the Pacific Ocean dominated by the Imperial Japanese Navy, the first step to guarantee safety for Australia and New Zealand was to establish a line of communication and supply via Hawaii and the islands of French Polynesia to Fiji and New Caledonia. Meanwhile, in an attempt to occupy all of New Guinea, Japanese troops landed, in early March, on the Lae – Salamaua coast on the north side of the rugged Owen Stanley Mountain Range. No road connects Lae through the mountains to Port Moresby on the south side of the range. Pushing inland the Japanese secured the Buna – Kokoda trail and came within sight of Port Moresby. Entrenched Australian troops with air support battled the enemy to a stand-still. By 16 September 1942 the enemy advance stalled and became a retreat; Allied forces gradually secured most of the island. On 6 November 1942 General MacArthur established his HQ at Port Moresby.

There was a secondary battle zone. The Japanese plan called for capture of Tulagi, an island 20 miles north of Guadalcanal, capital of Great Britain's Solomon Islands Protectorate. This secondary assault was to establish a base to support the invasion and capture of Port Moresby by sea and strengthen the defense of Rabaul. The Japanese Special Naval Landing Force plan to take Port Moresby had to be scuttled because, as the result of the Battle of the Coral Sea, two large Japanese aircraft carriers, which were to provide air cover for the landing, were severely damaged; one returned to Japan for repair the other to Truk atoll. This was a fortunate turn of events. Those carriers were not available to join Vice Admiral Nagumo's First Carrier Task Force in the fateful Battle of Midway.

Ultimately, the Japanese strong-hold at Lae–Salamaua was cleared and Port Moresby became a major American base. Rabaul was kept under constant siege while the Marines landed at Guadalcanal. During that campaign Japanese Naval forces, in a futile attempt to reinforce Guadalcanal, sent ships down the inter-island channel sailors called the "slot." Most were sunk in "Iron bottom" Bay. For the rest of the war Rabaul was effectively by-passed and eventually surrendered.

"Ducimus" . . ."We Lead". . . On 19 June 1941 the 22nd BG officially adopted their Latin motto. It became true in-fact when six B-26s of the 19th BS lead the Group's first combat mission 5 April 1942, to Rabaul. The 19th BS could rightly claim the full motto . . ." Ducimus ceteri sequuntur" – "We lead, others follow." The 22nd BG love affair with the B-26 began much earlier when the first four ships off the Martin Aircraft production line were delivered to them, 22 February 1941 at Langley Field, Virginia.

22nd Bomb Group Association members unveil memorial dedicated to 22nd BG airmen lost in Southwest Pacific combat 1942-45. L to R – R. McCutcheon, M. Edmonds, T. Dewan, W. Dewan, J. Wells – at *Charters Towers,* Queensland, Australia, 9/22/2012.

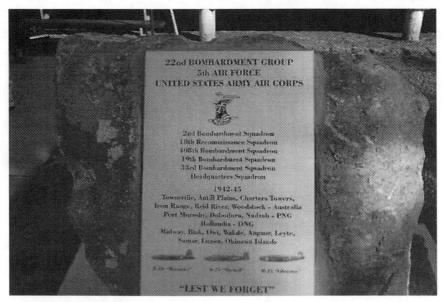

Lest We Forget – 22nd Bomb Group Memorial – *Charters Towers*, Queensland, Australia.

Content Scenario

"She has a personality all her own," said a proud combat crewman as we approached his airplane parked on a nearby hardstand. He was talking about his bold B-26 Marauder, "She's a thoroughbred – sleek and sassy – poised at the starting-gate ready to go – *look-out below!*" I sensed a kinship of affection known only to men who risk their lives in combat aboard this marvelous flying machine.

I also sensed a story yet untold. Perhaps it's the name on the nose that gives her life or maybe it's the anonymous production number, 40 -1436, on the tail. "I flew old 1436 today," said a pilot. "She's our 'Mystery Ship' – she's been smashed up twice and shot down once, it's a *mystery* the old clunk keeps flying." Not so to the nameless ground crew who service her; they are the quiet people of our story, working miracles with no glamour, no glory but with galleons of grit they're determined to keep 'em in the air. Another Marauder-man, in a philosophical mood, sensed an element of romance in her form and function. He mused, "40 – 1427 arrived back at sunset after its overhauling at the Air Depot," he said, "all paint removed – she's silver – positively beautiful to look at – graceful and shiny – ready to seduce young men in the wild blue yonder."

"My first real 'kick' out of flying came when I flew a Boeing P-12 after graduating from Kelly," commented Lt. Frank Allen of the 22nd BG. "My next big 'kick' came out of flying the Martin B-26." This casual comment by Lt. Frank Allen describes, in a sense, the Army Air Corps' switch from bi-planes to monoplanes. (The P-12 was the last pursuit bi-plane, flown by the army and navy well into the 1930s.) In another sense it symbolizes the – 'kick' – visionary military and aviation leaders had when asked to create a state-of-the-art 'battle ready' Army Air Corps.

Our story is also an informal mini history of the 22nd Bombardment Group recorded in a straight-shootin' frontier fashion by pilot, 1st Lt. Frank S. Allen, navigator 1st Lt. Merrill Thomas Dewan and by pilot 1st Lt. James P. Muri. The 22nd BG was the first US medium bomber group to enter combat, 5 April 1942, flying an untamed, fresh off the drawing board airplane. In less than a year the plane and people became a legend. This is also the story of one man's search for the best way to launch navy torpedoes from an army airplane. Let's look at the beloved but much maligned B-26 –"the Widow Maker."

Aircraft design took a giant leap forward when Glenn L. Martin's Model 179 (later to be known as the B-26) made her maiden flight, November 25, 1940, at the Middle River Airport, Baltimore, Maryland. It was a cool day with scattered clouds and a refreshing breeze.

A group of proud Martin employees gathered on the ramp to watch their new airplane warm-up. A front office PR man commented, "She's proud and potent," – "and pretty too," piped-up a young secretary. "Handsome," corrected an engineer standing near-by.

Tall and slim, the fuselage viewed straight-on, was a perfect circle like a fine cigar. Two under-wing motors promised full-blast-power ready to challenge the sky. With stubby wings her speed rivaled pursuit planes. The Army Air Corps dream had come true. They had their 300 mile per hour bomber.

In the air, test pilots soon learned her flight characteristics were dicey and unforgiving. But in the hands of an accomplished pilot she was a lady willing to carry her load with strength and dignity. She was ready for battle and planners said, **"The B-26 Goes to War!"**

Those same planners, with an eye for beauty, noticed the B-26 was shaped like a torpedo. It was inevitable that someone would notice the resemblance and suggest a "sea-going" role for this proud bird, launching torpedoes; sort-of a flying PT boat. Imaginative flag officers heard the word, gave it some thought, and said, "Hell, let's try it!" – Thus – we have our extended story.

To get the challenging project off the ground a "designated" torpedo-pilot with "fix-it" skills was needed. The weapon was a 2,000 pound naval aerial torpedo. Someone with weapons savvy was needed. 1st Lt. Frank S. Allen, Jr. was the obvious choice. He had a life-long interest in firearms, was a skilled sharpshooter with a built-in "fix-it" talent. Allen's flight of four B-26s had worked successfully with Admiral John "Slew" McCain at North Island, San Diego, patrolling his vast western sea frontier. (That story will be told later.) In fact, Lt. Allen's flight performed so well with the navy that Admiral McCain wanted to keep the B-26s and give the army all of his PBYs.

Our story is more than a *torpedo-toting-tale.* There is a "back story" about the 22nd BG – Bombardment Group, at Langley Field, Virginia, mobilizing in record time, 16 hours, on December 7th, flying across the continent, shipping planes to Hawaii, and then island hopping across the Pacific to Brisbane, Australia, thence, to up-country jungle strips where their battle sorties helped stop the Japanese invasion of Australia.

To complete the picture we look at B-26 torpedo tactics from the Aleutians in Alaska, the Battle of Midway and the final chapter at New Caledonia, on the Coral Sea, where planned torpedo runs faded away in favor of B-25 "skip-bombing." B-26 Marauders had proven their worth, had battled the vaunted "Zeros" to a stand-off and were now banished to North Africa and the ETO (European Theater of Operations) where they will chalk-up another proud record, (a story for another time). For the rest of this story we turn to 1st Lt. Merrill T. Dewan's *Red Raider Diary.* We are privileged to have excerpts from his writing which vividly portrays grim living conditions at jungle strips, at Port Moresby on New Guinea, squadron camaraderie between missions and air battles with enemy Zero fighters over the

Coral Sea. His poignant, sometimes sentimental diary entries are like passages from Michener's *Tales of the South Pacific;* they are honest, compassionate – straight from the heart.

For a spectacular opening, 1st lt. James P. Muri tells his story – about his first – and his last – combat mission. He happened to be holding in Hawaii, perhaps because of mechanical problems, but the timing couldn't have been better for commandeering his B-26, installing an untried weapons system and sending Jim and three other B-26 crews to participation in the Battle of Midway – historians agree this was the turning point of the Pacific war. Lt. Muri's action at low wave-top level decoyed enemy fighters from above and gave high flying Navy dive bombers time to target and destroy all four Japanese aircraft carriers. Visions of Jim's dash along the enemy's flight deck were a publicity bonanza. Like Doolittle's Tokyo raid it boosted "Home-front" enthusiasm, hope and confidence and inspired future flight crews.

Cover Story

Lt. James Muri – Buzzing *Akagi's* Flight Deck

"It popped up like a bird flushed from a nesting bush," said Commander Matsuo Fuchida, survivor of the Imperial Japanese Navy aircraft carrier *Akagi*. His 'bird' was Lt. Muri's B-26 just completing its torpedo run to sink his ship and now desperate to escape pursuing Zero fighters. "My memory of the action," recalls the Commander, "The plane was poised over the end of the flight deck looking for a way to go." The open deck of the *Akagi*, was like a peaceful glorious meadow, all guns pointing out away from the deck, and the Zeros remained silent fearful of strafing their own deck. Commander Fuchida wondered, "Would that 'bird' dare violate the Admiral's sacred space?"

The answer came like a thunder-clap, Lt. Muri made his move, "Susie-Q" – at full throttle – came charging down the deck, nose gun blazing, white clad sailors scurrying for cover. As it passed, Commander Fuchida glimpsed the big white star. "It looked like a Kabuki actor's all-white classic make-up – the demon head." A whimsical thought crossed his mind – this is no drama-theater, this deck is not a stage, and yet here we are, on the restless sea, witnessing a real-life drama." Artist: Jack Fellows captured that drama – that impossible deck-dash – shown on our cover.

1st Lt. James P. Muri (Norwegian for "glorious meadow") was

marking time at Hickam Field, Hawaii. His buddies of the 18th BS (Bombardment Squadron) had started island-hopping, atoll to atoll, on 12 April, across the Pacific to Australia. Why he and 1st Lt. Herbert C. Mayes were held back is not known; perhaps it was a maintenance issue. Meanwhile other B-26 ships, equipped with long range fuel tanks, were arriving in Hawaii. Captain Collins and Lt. Watson of the 69th BS arrived 22 May. Earlier in the month, May 4 – 8, the Battle of the Coral Sea, had played out like a textbook 'proving ground' experiment testing Carrier-to-Carrier warfare – airplanes replacing battleship big guns. Admiral Nimitz, with information provided by the broken Japanese Naval Operational Code, called JN-25b, knew the Battle of Midway was afoot. To out-smart Admiral Yamamoto's grand plan he would use all manner of weaponry including Army's B-26s carrying Navy's torpedoes.

News of Lt. Frank Allen's successful torpedo testing in Perth, Australia, had impressed higher authority so B-26s at Hickam Field were commandeered for the mission. Navy torpedo experts swarmed over the planes hastily rigging release mechanisms to the keel of the bombers. Pilots were told when a torpedo is attached under the belly there would be only a scant 4 inches clearance between the weapon and runway pavement. They were given rudimentary instructions on how to drop the "tin fish" and during the last 10 days of May, Captain James F. Collins, 1st Lt. William S. Watson, 1st Lt. .James P. Muri, 1st Lt. Herbert C. Mayes, practiced torpedo launching. Then they flew 1,100 miles to Midway Island. Waiting on the island was Navy Torpedo Eight detached from carrier *Hornet* flying six new TBF – Avengers. This *ad hoc* force would soon meet Vice Admiral Chuichi Nagumo's Japanese aircraft carrier armada.

All assets: land planes and carrier aircraft, were deployed on Midway 2 June 1942. It is said, and photos support the story, Army flyers, in order 'to stand-out' from Naval aviators, all sported trim Errol Flynn swash-buckler mustaches. On June 4th pilots and crews were on standby at 03:15 hour. There was no formal briefing. A Navy intelligence officer simply told them to "Fly out on a heading of 295 degrees about 190 miles and sink ships." The B-26s took off at 06:15. 1st Lt. James P. Muri was flying in the tail position of the four-plane diamond formation. Captain James F. Collins led, 1st Lt. Herbert C. Mayes was on the left wing, and 1st Lt. William S Watson was on the right. They were following six slow-moving Navy TBF, Avengers whose maximum speed was 205 mph. On the heels of the TBFs, at 07:05, "We were slicing through the Japanese fleet formation." At 07:07 *Akagi* commences firing at torpedo- carrying planes, "Boy, were we surprised! It seemed as though every ship had burst into flames, they were firing everything even the big battleship 16-inch batteries. Within seconds the water in front of us erupted in plumes, solid columns of water where shells hit. We slid past them." Dropping down to 200 feet above the waves the marauding B-26s pressed on. A swarm of Mitsubishi M6A "Zero" fighters jumped them. The fighters had been drawn down to sea level from high altitude Combat Air Patrol, CAP, fleet protection leaving the upper sky wide open. They were on the water to destroy torpedo planes. By 07:15 the B-26s completed their torpedo runs. The *Akagi*, at flank speed, dodged all torpedoes. Lt Muri had carried his torpedo run to within 800 yards of the carrier. At full speed "balls to the wall," he was closing fast on his massive target. The *Akagi*, turned evasively and the torpedo missed. Suddenly she loomed large directly ahead. In a split-second Muri's only option was to "buzz the beast."

Jim recalls: "I could see all the guns were pointing out, away from the deck. That was the safest place to be. So I lifted "Susie-Q" slightly over the ship's bow and skimmed down the deck. If I lowered the gear we would have rolled the whole length." His son James said, "All 42 surviving members of the air attacks, Army and Navy, were awarded the Distinguished Service Cross, DSC, for Valor. 14, who perished, including Mayes and Wilson, were given the award posthumously." The torpedo run story and Jim's 'barnstorming buzz' caught the imagination of Air Corps public relations so they brought Jim state-side on a speaking tour to boost morale. "I don't think he minded one bit not flying another mission," said his son Jim, "Midway was his first – and his last mission." Shortly after his brazen dash, he was joined by Collins, who had ducked into a cloud to escape the Zeros; later a lone surviving TDF joined their retreat in the haze to Midway Island. After landing, over 500 holes were counted in Jim's plane. Both Marauders were so badly damaged they were written off and dumped into the lagoon.

Meanwhile carriers *Yorktown*, *Enterprise* and *Hornet* launched aircraft including SBD – Dauntless dive bombers each carrying a 1,000 pound bomb. SBD (V-6) from *Enterprise* arrived on the scene almost undetected at 14,000 ft. altitude at 10:20. The Zero CAP was not there, they were busy on the deck dealing with the low flying torpedo planes; the sky overhead was undefended the carriers were naked and exposed to high flying dive bombers. In the excitement of spotting the Japanese fleet, the leading group of SBDs targeted the nearest carrier *Kaga* and pushed over into their dive. Three other SBDs saw what was happening and shifted their aim to the flagship *Akagi*. Screaming down in a steep 70 degree dive they released their 1,000 pounders at 1,500 feet. One bomb scored a direct hit. The other two were near misses, the *Akagi* was doomed. Meanwhile, north of the action, SBDs from the *Yorktown* hit the carrier *Soryu* and left it ablaze. The attack was all over in a matter of five minutes; three of Nagumo's carriers, *Akagi*, *Kaga*, *Hiryu*, were wracked with explosions and swept with flames stem to stern – sinking. The forth carrier, *Soryu*, was crippled and was scuttled the next day. In addition to losing four carriers Nagumo lost the heavy cruiser, *Mikuma*. By contrast, the U.S. losses were one carrier, the *USS Yorktown,* and the destroyer *USS Hammann.* The *Yorktown* had been heavily damaged and the destroyer was alongside assisting in salvage and rescue when they were both torpedoed by a Japanese submarine. Historians agree The Battle of Midway was the crucial turning point in the Pacific. It stopped Japanese westward expansion and changed the course of the war.

Introduction – This Is War

This is 1ˢᵗ Lt. Frank S. Allen's Story

Heavy black smoke rose high over Battleship Row as enemy bombers found their targets in the early morning surprise attack on Pearl Harbor, Hawaii; meanwhile, six time-zones east in Hampton, Virginia, Langley Field flyers and families were enjoying a pastoral Sunday afternoon, December 7ᵗʰ 1941.

1ˢᵗ Lt. Franklin S. Allen and his wife Jeanne had slept late after enjoying a rousing Saturday night dance at the Officers Club followed by a "night-cap" stop at Chris Herron's apartment in Hampton and finally a stop at Major Lauback's house back on the post. "We finally got to bed at 7 A.M. Sunday morning fully expecting a nice quiet day to recover."

The scene was rudely shattered when fellow B-26 pilot, Al Moye, bounded in and shouted up the stairway, "They've bombed Pearl Harbor!"

Frank recalled, "Instead of leaping out of bed all excited, we both thought he was kidding." On second thought, Al was not known as the Squadron jokester.

"If you don't believe me," shouted Al, "come down, listen to the radio!"

Radio station WWDC – 1450 kcs, broadcasting from Washington DC, was heard loud and clear in Hampton. Regular programs were being interrupted with news bulletins. The reports were pretty confused and excited.

The airfield family housing neighborhood remained routinely quiet. Officers and wives were glued to their radios pondering the news. In an air of disbelief they were all wondering – what's next? For the Allens –"what's next?" Was a routine drive into Hampton, to Joe's Deli on King Street, for one of his fabulous homemade hamburgers. As they approached the gate the barrier remained down. The MP on duty, Sergeant Stacy, recognized the Allens, saluted and said, "Sorry, sir, no one is allowed off the base." What? Thought Frank, we can't go get a hamburger? Turning to Jeanne he said, **"This is War!"**

Returning home, Frank recalls. "I remember not being especially surprised and realized finally, we were about the only bombardment organization really ready for war – or were we ready? We did have 13 B-26s in the squadron – primed and nearly ready – I think."

*Editor's Note: Lt. Allen recounts his activities over recent months and realizes, without surprise, each event, though often isolated, was part of a grand preparedness puzzle which now comes together – a historic panorama – and he is in it. To set the stage please see – **Appendix A.***

At home after listening to the radio for a few minutes, I got into my car and drove down to the hangar to see what was going on. No one was there except for a few sleepy guards. The airplanes sat around, many of them in various states of disassembly for repair and one thing or another. I thought at the time if the Japanese had attacked Langley Field they would have caught us flatfooted.

Back at the house, Jeanne whipped up something to eat and we listened to the radio for awhile. Finally the phone rang and Major Haskins, our squadron commander was calling, "Come down to the hangar at once." I figured it was about time we did something. From that phone call on, I wasn't to get more than an hour's sleep or more than a sandwich to eat for four days.

At the hangar we had a brief meeting and we were to put all the airplanes in commission, install turrets in three of them – that alone is normally a two day job – load all ships with ammunition, pack our

own bags, and be ready to leave for somewhere at dawn. We worked all night, harder than any of us had before.

I commanded B-Flight consisting of Johnny Ewbanks, Aleron Larson and John Cooper. As I write this now *(mid-May 1942)* Cooper is the only one left still flying with me. We had a helluva time getting the ammunition. Finally, sixteen hours later at 4 AM, we were done. I went back to the house for a sandwich and about 30 minutes sleep. Jeanne had packed my bags for me and did a wonderful job. Quite a job, packing for an aviator who can't take more than he can carry, destined to go "somewhere."

Jeanne and I drove back to the hangar at 5 AM. All of the wives were there, most of them crying. I'm glad Jeanne didn't. It was a rather dramatic way to go to war. We had eleven airplanes ready – the other two were to come the next day. Finally we were ready to take off. I kissed Jeanne good-by not knowing when I would ever see her again. I fully expected to be fighting in the next few days.

Chapter One

Langley Field – Muroc Lake

We took off and circled the field once in formation. That would be the last time we would ever have that many airplanes in the air at once in the states.

My crew that morning consisted of myself, my copilot Willy Vroom, navigator Noel Wright, bombardier Chuck Eberly, crew chief Sgt. "Doc" Harris, radio operator Sgt. Holden, gunner Private Jordan, and tail gunner Private Brakefield. Our first stop was Memphis, Tennessee, where we grabbed a hamburger and refueled. We had a helluva time refueling as a P-39 squadron had landed ahead of us and got to the pump first. I remember the P-39 CO was a classmate of mine, and although neither of us knew it then, he was to give me top cover on a later mission and to shoot down a Zero that was making an attack on my ship.

Our next stop was to be Albuquerque, New Mexico. That hop was a tough one. I was so tired I could only keep my eyes open for about thirty minutes at a time. Then I'd have to turn the ship over to Willy who was about in the same shape. Of all the damn times, the auto pilot had to cut out! With darkness and Oklahoma approaching, the wing men began to straggle, and it was an effort to keep track of them. One of the boys in the lead flight straggled back and got lost over Texas – but finally followed the light line and picked us up about 50 miles from Albuquerque. (***Editor's note***: *As early as 1926 the*

CAA positioned rotating beacons 15 to 20 miles apart along designated airway corridors. On a clear night they were a comforting sight blinking every 10 seconds, often seen four in a row. By 1930, 14,500 miles were lighted.) None of us had ever been to Albuquerque before, but the map showed that the field was located in a sort of a bowl, the edges of which were 10,000 foot mountains. The formation almost broke up a few times. Flying formation at night for long periods is a difficult chore at best, but as tired as we were it was a nightmare.

We arrived over the field shortly after midnight and landed in a sort of a race for the field. The formation broke up their traffic pattern, and between the flight leaders calling their men, and the tower people going crazy, it was quite a landing. However, we got in with no accidents, which was something. We parked the airplanes and were immediately bundled off to some barracks for a couple hours of sleep.

In the morning some of the ships needed parts. Carson lost his turret dome over Arkansas for one thing. As luck would have it there was a wrecked B-26 on the field which had been there for about 10 days. It had been ferried by someone in the group on its way to Sacramento, California to be winterized, and then it was to be flown to Alaska. For us it posed as an "on the spot Air Corps supply." Our sergeants approached it gleefully with wrenches in hand only to be met by the Post Commander, a full Colonel, who said, "Not one part of that airplane was to be touched." Haskins drew him over to one side to argue, and the men went in and stripped the airplane clean. The Colonel was furious, but what did we care. We were going to war, and brass hats were just so many "Japs" to be done away with. That was the beginning of my firm conviction that 90 percent of our hold-over high ranking officers were gumming up the war effort.

Anyway, the next day about 8 AM, off we went again and after flying through lots of lousy weather, finally arrived at Muroc Lake, California, in the afternoon. It was here we learned the rumor we had heard at Albuquerque was true. Col. Lewis and Major Layback were dead. They were taking off from Biggs Field, El Paso, when their left engine failed. Apparently they made the old mistake of turning into the dead engine trying to get back to the field, and the inevitable result happened. The dead wing went down, and they couldn't get it up before they hit the ground.

Our group commander and group executive officer gone and the war only a few days old! How much better this war would have been if they could have lived! I have never met two finer or more competent officers! Major Haskins, who had a lot of ideas, but was a boastful braggart sort of man, overly aware of his own importance, took command of the group. From that day group morale and spirit seemed to sink.

The first few days at Muroc were a nightmare. For all we knew the Japs might be set to attack Los Angeles or San Francisco, and we were the only bombardment force on the Pacific coast at the time. Muroc was a helluva place. You land on the floor of a huge dry lake which is about 20 miles long and 8 wide. By the time we had our airplanes parked, it was night again, and we were scattered all over the lake – not knowing where we were – and of course it started raining. The pay-off came when we were sitting, waiting in the airplane, when the truck that had been sent to pick us up ran into the tail of the airplane. I gave the driver terrible tongue lashing not realizing that he was about as tired as we were. Fortunately the tail wasn't severely damaged. We were hauled over to the main camp and were fed some cold fried spam and coffee. That was the beginning of a very strong rift between the Armour Company and me. How they ever talked the Army into ever buying that damn stuff I'll never know, but I wish the Armour family had to live for weeks on it.

We were ordered to load with bombs. We got off to a bad start. After working for several hours loading 500 pound bombs they changed their minds, and switched to loading 300 pounders. Half the ships didn't have their loading gear. No one person knew where half the airplanes were parked and the rain did not abate. About two in the morning we were led to some tents which were magnificently furnished with wet straw and two blankets per man. At least the tent didn't leak and we were too tired to care much about anything. The next day several men were taken to a hospital suffering from exhaustion and pneumonia. Well, the Japs didn't show up that day, and that afternoon Major Haskins told me that Admiral McCain down at North Island, San Diego needed some support, and I was to take my flight and go down there in the morning.

Chapter Two

Navy – North Island Patrols

After riding around in the back of a 2 ½ ton truck in the rain and muck of Muroc, North Island was heaven.

We landed and parked, December 15, 1941, and immediately a brand new station wagon met me and whisked me off to the Admiral. I looked like hell. No sleep, no clothes change, no shave, no food to amount to anything for four days, and suddenly I found myself sitting in a big easy chair facing an Admiral. He was swell. His first words were, "Thank God you've come, boy." He then rang for an attendant who brought in some coffee. After the coffee he told me. "All I have to defend the Naval Base is one squadron of three, four-engine Consolidated flying boats and a squadron of Catalinas. I saw why he was so happy we had arrived to help patrol his western sea frontier. I was introduced to brass-hats who promptly started asking me how far we could cruise with how many bombs, etc. I wasn't much help, because our fuel consumption runs were still very incomplete. We had never flown any tests with full bomb loads, but I finally said I'd try to give them 1,500 statute miles with 2,700 pounds of bombs at an average speed of 190 mph. I over did it a bit, but we did run some missions with that load.

I rather timidly pointed out we were ready to go then, but would it be all right to get a couple hours sleep and a little food? The Admiral asks why and I told him. He immediately said, "Hell, boy,

I'll give you two days to rest up and be ready." That sounded like a reprieve from the electric chair. I got the enlisted men fixed up in the main sailors' barracks, and the rest of us went to the Junior Officers Quarters. What a place! Magnificent rooms with big beds and mattresses and orderlies to clean the place up, plus a bar, a lounge room. About a block down the street was the mess. Negro attendants were bringing in steaks and green vegetables on silver serving trays. Wow! We all went to bed, and the following morning got ourselves organized.

We were assigned a Navy lieutenant to act as liaison officer and procurer of Navy supplies. The first problem was bomb loading. We decided to carry two Navy 1,100 pound bombs in the front bay. The auxiliary bomb bay tank hold 2,500 extra gallons of gas and a 500 pound bomb in the back bomb bay. We took up the entire flight that afternoon for a little formation practice and a look at the nearby auxiliary landing fields. The Naval lieutenant had never flown in an Army plane before and was quite surprised to see a bombardment plane fly faster than even their F4F Grumman fighter. He was even more surprised to see me glide in at 145 mph and land at 120 mph.

That evening we loaded the bombs, and I checked in with the staff to see what the plans were. After some discussion we decided that one of our ships would go out each day on patrol along with the PBYs and the four engine boats. Two B-26s would stand by on instant alert, and the fourth would be off for maintenance, and the crew would be off for 24 hours. I decided to fly the first mission, a rather short one of about 1,000 miles. Besides, with our bomb and gas load, the total weight was 34,600 pounds or 4,200 pounds overload. Seeing as how that great an overload had never been flown before, I should try it the first time.

So the next morning I took off. I had no difficulty taking off but my climb was a bit slow. As the mission was only 1,000 miles with no climbing or fighter combat expected, I cruised around 225 mph the whole mission. This was a mistake! The Navy got the idea that we could always cruise that fast. The next day Eubanks got the mission, and it was for 1,500 miles. After computing and checking our gas curves, I told Johnny to cruise at 27 inched manifold pressure and hold 1700 rpm, never realizing, with that load, that wouldn't be enough power to hold the ship in the air. Johnny did what he was told almost too well. He didn't change his power settings until he found himself at 50 feet above the water at 150 mph and still going down. Johnny was an hour overdue on his Estimated Time of Arrival, (ETA). And we spent some unhappy moments until we spotted him coming in at almost dusk. He had been in the air nearly eight hours at an average speed of 185 mph. That night I suggested that a 1,200 mile mission would be more in keeping. The Admiral was pleased even with that.

Lt. Cooper had the third mission and about 580 miles out from San Diego damned if he didn't run into a full-grown Japanese submarine almost fully surfaced. The Navy liaison office that was along said it looked as big as a destroyer. Cooper went on the run at 1,000 feet and Stoneking, the enlisted bombardier whom we had just barely finished training when the war began, opened the doors. On they went and actually got directly over the sub, which was submerging fast, but no bomb was dropped. Coop screamed at Stoneking to drop, but it was too late. He whipped the ship around in a vertical turn to make a new run, but it was too late. The sub was gone. Stoneking, it seems, didn't drop because he suddenly remembered, that in training, he was told that dropping a bomb that size at 1,000 feet would also blow you out of the air; which was true of a bomb with an instantaneous fuse dropped on land. No one ever told him that you could go as low as 500 feet over water. Of all the times he had to remember a no-no! If he had dropped his two 1,100 pound bombs they would have blown that sub right out of the water; even a miss of 200 feet would have sunk it. Live and learn. The Navy was disgusted. We were disgusted. I expect the Admiral had a few salty words, not at us, but at lack of luck. Everyone was pretty unhappy about the whole thing.

The next day, luck seemed to have changed, a patrolling PBY spotted a sub-mother ship with two subs refueling. They started their bomb run but the mother ships' guns shot back putting a hole in the PBYs hull. The PBY turned away and radioed for help, but our B-26 had already returned to its base. Another PBY in the area answered the call but were unable to locate it because of bad weather and approaching darkness. Neither episode was ever made public, which was a good thing. It would have unnerved the excitable Pacific Coast even more, and neither episode reflected any credit upon the Army or the Navy. The Navy stopped kidding us about our botched effort. They had one of their own.

I was on alert one afternoon when the phone rang and operations gave us the latitude and longitude of a suspected enemy sub. Fortunately everyone was on hand and we were off the ground in five minutes, but not without anxious puckering moments. I left my window open which created a cockpit tornado; one of the prop controls was left on "manual" and the prop promptly ran away, all this while we rolled merrily down the runway. All was corrected and we were up. Operations plotted the coordinates which put the sub about 20 miles from San Diego. When we arrived, we found a good many oil slicks which may have indicated the presence of an enemy sub. A friendly destroyer and submarine in the vicinity came over, and I dropped a smoke bomb on the suspect area; they depth charged but found no confirming evidence. After about an hour's search, I closed the Bombay doors and started home. When bombardier Beverly went to put the safety pins back in the bombs he discovered that the tail vanes of the lower bomb had become partially unscrewed which pulled out the arming wire from the tail fuse causing the pin to fly out, and thus we had a fully armed live bomb on his hands. As the fuse is pretty sensitive, rather than remove it, we just opened the door, dropped the whole thing into the ocean and came on home.

Regarding the bombs, the Navy 1,100 pound bombs were a little longer than our Army bombs and thus their nose fuse came dangerously close to the front of the bomb bay. I tried to get the Army regional supply officer to get me some Army bombs. He flubbed around for a day with no results, so I put in an emergency call to Muroc Lake, the main bomb dump. In the morning eight 2,000 pounders and 16, 1,100 pounders arrived by trucks which had driven all night across the mountains to get them to us. Best action we ever got.

The Navy was also fantastically cooperative with us. In a way I guess they had to be, for we were the only first line combat airplanes in the area other than the First Pursuit Group, also based at North Island. We had a full hangar to ourselves which was equipped with luxurious offices, machine shop, etc. I finally moved the enlisted men right into the spare room in the hangar, which was more than satisfactory to everyone. One incident that stands out was when one of the ships was grounded because of seriously leaking intake manifold gaskets. As this was the first time the big Pratt & Whitney 2,000 horse power engines had ever been used on the coast, there were no replacement parts out here, and it began to look as if we were going to have them flown from the factory at Hartford, Conn.

Things were looking bad when suddenly the P&W Tech-Representative I had called in from nearby Consolidated Aircraft, had a brainstorm. He went to the Navy overhaul plant, had them tear down a 1,250 horsepower P&W engine and in the blower section somewhere was a seal identical to the one we needed. We put them in that night and were ready to go in the morning. The entire time we were at North Island we kept all four B-26s in commission with no spare parts and only the combat crew chiefs to work on them. We had crisis after crisis, but every time the Navy's overhaul plant would come to the rescue and make the needed part or rig up some kind of substitute. Once we ran out of hydraulic fluid, and as ours was a special type, it was not readily procurable. So the Navy chemist came to the fore, analyzed the stuff, and overnight manufactured us a supply. Their service was almost unbelievable. If the Army ever gets one-half as organized and as efficient as the Navy was at North Island, we'll win this war a lot faster. Of course they were operating from a fixed base, whereas we have to haul our stuff around with us wherever we go.

Chapter Three

Muddy Muroc – March Field

After nearly two weeks of sheer joy, Admiral McCain called me in one afternoon and with a long face said, "Major Haskins had been screaming for you to return to Muroc and had gotten 4th Air Force to order you back. I'd like to send all my PBYs to the Army and keep your B-26s." he slapped the desk, "You've been doing the patrol jobs in half the time of the PBYs with twice the bomb load." I didn't want to go back to Muroc either. Once you get the taste of being your own boss, it's hard to go back to your old job. However it had been a wonderful break for us. On the off days I had sent the pilot and copilot of the off ship out on a PBY 4 engine boat in order that they might brush up on their navigation. Also, we had several ship recognition classes using models. One thing, we had certainly learned how to do coastal patrol and everyone's general ability had improved. I guess really the biggest advantage was that, for the first time, we had a fairly accurate idea of just how we could fly with various load conditions. That information was to help us tremendously later on.

Before we left, however, Haskins wired me to make a survey of all the landing fields in Southern California that might be suitable for B-26 use. The Navy, in an effort to get us to locate near San Diego, insisted on my looking over a little field about ten miles north of the city which they were using for a Marine fighter strip. Against my better judgment, I squeezed into the field. I just did get in using full brakes the length of the field. It turned out the darn thing was 2,200 feet long. Fortunately the wind was blowing about 20 mph, or I never would have gotten out. As it was I went through the tops of some trees at the end. That was the last time I ever let anyone talk me into anything connected with flying a B-26. I landed at a couple of fields at Long Beach and at Mines Field where they were working on the B-19, It got close to lunch, so I decided I'd go over to Douglas's Santa Monica plant and surprise my parents for lunch as my home is only a few miles from there.

I did just squeeze into Douglas, and even if they didn't have the factory there, it wouldn't have been suitable for our use. However, some fat-faced Army colonel came up and wanted to know just why I was landing at Douglas. I told him, quite honestly, that I was inspecting fields for B-26 use. He got quite indignant that we would even consider Douglas for a tactical field, which I realized all along no one had any intentions of doing, but he was so nasty about it that I finally told him that if I thought this field was satisfactory for our use we would darn well use it and that was fine as far as I was concerned. He screamed something about phoning Washington and ran into his office. I hope he did. He would have sounded silly saying some 1st Lt. In a B-26 was going to put in a group of 60 B-26s at the Douglas plant. Anyway, Mother finally arrived and we went to lunch. Father came in from town, and after we finished lunch we went back to the plant. Father had wanted a few 50 caliber cartridges for use as a display in his business. However they wouldn't let Mother or Father in the plant so I went through and got about 20 cartridges and gave them to one of the factory executives who knew Father and said he would give them to him. I took off and went back to San Diego. Father later told me that the minute I took off this goddamn Colonel came up and took the cartridges away from the executive because I was allegedly giving away government property. I felt like going back and bombing the Douglas plant with a handful of cartridges. Some people are born bastards, but a good many Colonels seem to acquire it when they get their eagles. Second Lieutenants and Generals are the easiest people to get along with.

The next day I returned to Muroc. I went on a couple of coastal patrols up to San Francisco and then came down with a bad cold. Eubanks borrowed my airplane for the next day's patrol and was forced down at Palm Springs because of weather. Because the field looked bad, he landed on a nearby road and the county had to build a road from where he stopped rolling over to the airport in order to get them off. While in Palm Springs the movie colony entertained them like visiting royalty . . . just my luck to be sick that day.

Muroc the next few days was horrible. It was freezing cold at night; a 40 mile an hour wind blew incessantly, constantly starting huge dust storms which covered everything with dust and sand. Everyone was coming down with flu and pneumonia and our maintenance was rapidly going to hell. The guards down on the lake were scared of their own shadow and one of them shot into the back of a truck loaded with men because the driver failed to hear the cry "halt." Fortunately, only one man was killed.

The food was terrible; mostly fried spam which I wouldn't even feed a starving dog. Christmas, 1942, was lovely. Instead of snowing it sleeted. The damn tents leaked. Someone in my tent got a few cans of beer somewhere and we huddled around a makeshift stove in our winter flying suits. We drank our beer. The stove was quite an invention. It consisted of a regulation G.I. tent stove but as fire wood was unobtainable, we converted it to oil. I found some fittings on a wrecked airplane and with the aid of a 5 gallon can and a soldering iron. I rigged up a device that would slowly feed oil into the stove. For fuel we used airplane engine oil mixed with a little 100 octane gasoline so it would burn better. One night I got a mixture from one of the sergeants that turned out to be mostly 100 octane. My first realization of this was when I commented on how swell the stove was working. Everyone thought I was a genius because no one else's burner had worked that well before. However, my worst fears were confirmed when the fire worked out of the stove up the hose connections up to the three gallon can and began burning on the outside of the can. In a minute we had a helluva fire on our hands, but finally we got it out with a blanket. We were never so enthusiastic about oil burners after that.

After Christmas things began to get a little more organized and at least we knew an hour before our patrol missions where we were going. Our missions were either down to the end of the Gulf of Mexico or down to San Diego, up to San Francisco and then back to Muroc. The weather was exceedingly lousy over the mountains with severe icing conditions at all times. This worried us more than anything else as we had no deicers and the B-26 has a very high wing loading as it is without ice adding to the weight. One of our ships apparently iced up on takeoff and crashed a little way from camp with a full load of bombs. This was our second fatal accident since the war began.

Inasmuch as we were supposed to be hunting submarines, Haskins decided we ought to investigate the possibility of carrying depth charges. So we flew up to San Francisco, and I dropped Haskins off at Hamilton Field and went to the Navy Field at Oakland. They had no depth bombs but did have some PBY depth charges. However, they were intended to be carried on the outside of a PBY wing and were dropped sideways with their long axis parallel with the wing. As they wouldn't fit cross-wise in our bomb bay I proposed that we put fins on one end and build up the other end with a cone and drop' em like a bomb. However, as that had never been tried before the Navy's ordinance officer was afraid the fuse, which was a delicate affair, might be damaged by the shock of hitting parallel to its axis rather than cross-wise as was intended. I found out that they had done just that at Pearl Harbor after the raid and it worked out OK. However, when I picked up Hawkins the next day at Hamilton he was full of some hot dope about going "somewhere" pretty soon, so we decided to forget the whole thing.

Chapter Four

Torpedo School – Coronado Bliss

Shortly after we returned from San Francisco the group got a wire from Washington to send one officer and 10 men down to San Diego Naval Torpedo School to learn all we could about naval torpedoes. That was the beginning of quite an episode in my flying career. But I'm getting ahead of my story, as about that time it was decided to move the group over to March Field as Muroc was getting untenable. Thank God for that. We packed up our stuff and prepared to take off. We had about 12 men and their baggage. We were taking off from a concrete strip that had been built just off the lake, as the lake was then a sea of mud due to the unusually heavy rains. I checked the controls in the usual fashion and took off.

When we were about 50 feet in the air Sgt. Holden called up on the intercom and in a very calm voice said, "Sir, the left engine in on fire." My mind was preoccupied with the bad weather that lay ahead and his calm statement didn't react as quickly as it should have so I pressed my mike button and replied, "Okay left engine is on fire." Then I suddenly realized what I had said! I look out the side window and sure enough the left engine was on fire! And how! Flame was pouring out of the engine nacelle and cowling was melting off like butter. I pulled back the left throttle immediately as the flames were eating into the firewall behind which lay the fuel lines, which were made of rubber.

My first impulse was to land straight ahead as I remembered what had happened to everyone else who had tried to get back with one engine. However, the ground ahead was pretty rough and I had a helluva load of men aboard. Fortunately I had my wheels and flaps up and was doing 170 mph. The left engine was still running although the fire had reduced somewhat with the throttle closed. So I squeezed out a very flat turn just off the ground and headed back towards the lake planning to land wheels up in the mud. I was then 25 feet in the air. My right engine was wide open and had about 165mph speed. Sgt. Holden wanted to pull the fire extinguisher on the left engine but I was afraid it would cut the engine out completely, and I wanted that engine in case I needed it, fire or no fire. When I got down opposite the runway, I decided to save the airplane, so I gave the bad engine full power, did a sharp 180 degree turn and let down the wheels. The wheels locked in place just as I hit. I cut the switches and hoped for the best. I was never so glad to get back on the ground in my life. By all rules of flying I should have never gotten away with it, and the next time it happens I'll land straight ahead – wrecked airplane or no wrecked airplane.

On inspection it seems that the exhaust stacks on the bottom two cylinders of the left engine had come off, and the tremendous exhaust flames had eaten off all the cowling on that side and had eaten half way into the fire wall right on the spot where the fuel line was. Another minute and the fuel line would have burned through and the airplane probably would have exploded. Somebody was looking out for me that day. Fortunately a wrecked airplane was nearby and the crew stripped the necessary parts from it and we took off for March Field the next morning. Incidentally that afternoon a flight from one of the other squadrons while crossing the mountains hit some very bad weather. Eight ships went on instruments through the pass and seven came out. They found the wreckage of the eighth not far from Big Bear Lake a couple of weeks later. Three crews gone and we still hadn't really gone into action yet. Rumors were flying pretty heavily by now that we were soon to be shipped overseas, so despite warnings from Haskins to the contrary I wired Jeanne to hop the next plane and come out. She did and I'll never regret that action.

I had only been at March for a day or two when Haskins told me I was leaving immediately for the torpedo school by army transport so once again I found myself at North Island; this time without an airplane. The Navy assigned me a boat and in a few minutes we were in San Diego harbor on our way to the destroyer base where the school was located. We were only allowed 10 days for a course that normally took three months or more. Fortunately they weren't rushed at the time so they gathered several old Chief Petty Officers who were their best instructors, and we started right in that afternoon. We were to go on a 24-hour basis, and I will say those instructors really worked on us.

Jeanne was due to arrive the next morning by air so the Navy gave me a station wagon to pick her up and the morning off to get settled. It was wonderful to see my wife again after leaving her that dreary Monday morning at Langley fully expecting not to see her again until after the war. We went over to Coronado and located a nice little apartment hotel. That short stay in Coronado was one of the happiest of my life. Several of the destroyer task force officers lived in Coronado and each morning a gig from the destroyer base came over to pick them up, so I rode to work along with them and came back in the evening the same way. The course was amazingly thorough despite the short time we had to learn about the torpedoes. A torpedo is one of the most complicated pieces of machinery ever built. It is small but its amazingly powerful engine involves extremely complicated plumbing to say nothing of the gyro controlled steering apparatus. Fortunately the 10 men we had selected to take the course learned unusually quickly and received not a little praise from the instructors for their adeptness. I spent three days at North Island learning from the experts there the science of torpedo tactics and working out a basic attack plan which would be suitable for our type of airplane. Knowing that so many major warships had been sunk by aerial torpedoes, plus my new understanding of its use, made me firmly convinced a well-coordinated approach should be the only way to attack naval units.

My plan of attack was one making full use of supporting aircraft. I have never believed any type of aircraft carrying torpedoes can come within range of anti-aircraft fire of large vessels and still effectively drop torpedoes. A torpedo attack must always be preceded by a high altitude attack to divert attention, and by a strafing attack by fast and maneuverable fighters to neutralize anti-aircraft fire long enough to give torpedo planes a chance to dart in close enough to launch their torpedoes and get out. The principle of a torpedo attack is to have at least six or more torpedo planes coming in from different directions on both sides of the ship and off the front quadrant. The idea is to lay a pattern of torpedoes in the water in such a way that no matter which way the ship may turn it will still be hit by one or more torpedoes. One hit by a torpedo is worth ten hits by bombs. An underwater explosion lets the water in.

The B-26 is remarkably suited for a torpedo plane primarily because it is heavily armed and can successfully beat off attacking fighters, plus the fact that it is fast and can get in and out of anti-aircraft gun range quickly. Our present Navy torpedo plane is certainly too vulnerable to enemy fighters as was shown at Midway, and is much too slow. Besides, because of its short range it must have a vulnerable carrier haul it around. A B-26 can haul a torpedo 600 miles from its land base and get home. Present torpedo planes are lucky if they can go 200 miles away. If you have good enough runways, to get off from, the B-26 radius of action can be increased to 750 miles by using extra fuel tanks.

During the torpedo course, one of our squadron's ships came into North Island on one engine. The crew was trucked back to March. After the course, I was sent a crew, and after a week's delay I took the ship up to Sacramento where it was to be dismantled prior to being shipped "somewhere." On the way up I went out of my way to fly where two and one half years before I had received my primary flight training. It was quite a thrill after having left the last time just barely qualified to fly a primary airplane to fly low over the field at 300 mph in the world's fastest, hottest bomber.

I returned by transport *(****Editor's. Note****: perhaps a Douglas C-47)* to March where Jeanne and I stayed at the Mission Inn in Riverside. Each day we would drive out to the field, even though we were doing no flying, to get the latest dope. The rumors were coming fast by now. We were going to Africa, Java, Australia, even Russia! Every day it was a different place. Mother and Father were swell and gave us one of their cars so we could get around. We drove to Arrowhead, to Palm Springs, into Los Angeles. Always we had to come back to check in. Finally, about the first of February it came. We were to be ready the next day to take the train for San Francisco. The sands of time were running short.

We tried not to think about it too much, but it wasn't easy. We boarded the train the next morning and all the wives followed us right up. We were whisked over to the San Francisco docks from the train station in buses, and there it was the ship, *USS Grant*. It wasn't just a rumor this time, because there it was. In less than an hour we had said good-by to our wives at the landing and boarded the boat which started pulling out almost immediately. Instead of sailing immediately, it pulled out into the bay and sat for two days while the convoy was being made up. Two battleships lay along side. We were all a little bit flattered to think that two battleships' were going to escort us "somewhere." ***Editor's note:*** *While the USS Grant is anchored in San Francisco Bay let's put 1ˢᵗ Lt. Frank Allen's narrative on hold while we explore Code Breaking, newspaper warning and preparedness in* ***Appendix B.***

Chapter Five

Troopship to Hawaii

On February 5, 1942, when we finally filed out through the Golden Gate the battleships were conspicuous by their absence.

The *USS Grant* was an old German liner of about 9,000 tons and had been taken over by the Army as a troop ship. At this time, however, it had been taken over by the Navy. There were about 1,000 of us aboard. The air echelon of our group, several hundred civilian employees and about 300 casual enlisted men. I was put in charge of the enlisted men as they had no officers with them. I occupied an extremely small room with Joe Warner, our squadron CO on A – Deck which was a break because the doors opened out onto the deck. The trip was more or less uneventful after we were told we were going to Hawaii. The convoy included a freighter loaded with some of our airplanes, a tanker loaded with gasoline, another ship loaded with nurses and soldiers and civilians, and a Navy freighter. We were escorted by two destroyers. We held classes in the morning. I gave a short course on ship recognition and torpedoes. I was kept busy most of the time with the enlisted men. They were pretty seasick most of the time, being packed like sardines in the forward hold. I had to organize them into sectors and put sergeants in charge in order to get them to keep the place clean and to get them out on the deck once in a while. I kept at them pretty rigorously on the clean living thing making them scrub the bulkheads and deck each day and insisting that they make their beds. The food wasn't bad and was served in three sittings in a small dining hall.

Our biggest thrill came at exactly 12:01 the morning of Friday the 13th of February. I was sound asleep in my upper berth when I was suddenly awakened by shouts and frantic whistling by our ship's whistle. I thought we had been torpedoed. When Joe threw open the state room door, all I could see were rockets being fired up by the freighter along side of us. I got my life vest on and started to be concerned about the whole thing, when my attention was diverted by what seemed at the time one of the funniest things had ever seen. Our cabin was located next to the main door to the after part of the ship. Each time the door was opened by a sailor running to his gun post a little light leaked out from a blue light in the companionway. Warner stopped the lead sailor and bawled him out for letting the light out. Then, as the sailors started out on the run again, each and every one of them tripped over a deck chair which had been carelessly left out on deck. Actually, under the circumstances, the situation wasn't funny at all, but I got laughing so hard the ship could have been under water and I wouldn't have known it. Pretty soon the destroyers got busy and the explosions of depth charges could be heard even through the din of all the whistling. We thought the ship along side had been hit because of all the rockets, but in the morning we found out they had spotted the wakes of three torpedoes headed for us; the nearest of the three passed within ten feet of our bow, so we were told.

That occurrence, plus the fact that we were getting restless made the voyage tedious. A few days later we had a happy ship when the low slopes of Molokai Island suddenly showed up out of the morning mist. We were also greeted by a B-17 and a B-18 which did a short submarine patrol. We finally pulled into Honolulu harbor where we disembarked and were loaded onto a funny little ancient narrow gauge railway and were hauled out to Hickam Field. What a shock that was. The train pulled right along side of the hangars, or what was left of them. Most of the debris was still lying around, having merely been pulled off the streets.

Chapter Six

Hawaii Interlude

This was the first time I had ever seen anything actually destroyed by enemy action, and it was a shock. It was hard to realize that this mess was once a great United States airfield like Langley Field only a little bigger and more modern. Most of the hangars were still standing twisted frames of steel and tin with gaping holes through them. It seemed as if nothing escaped. Even the fire house was completely riddled with cannon shell holes. The concrete curbs along the back of the hangar line were shattered and broken. Wrecked B-17s, P-40s, B-18s and a B-10 were still lying along side of the hangars, giving vivid and mute testimony to the effectiveness of that Jap raid. It was not a pretty sight for an American citizen, and especially an Army aviator, to see. Back from the hangar lines were immense new barracks with the upper stories burned out. Hundreds died in those barracks. A little further down was the drill field. Over a hundred died on that field, because they couldn't believe that those silver planes were actually shooting at them. They were American soldiers on American soil, especially one of the most heavily defended areas America has. Fortunately I didn't see Pearl Harbor for several days. I had time to get prepared for that.

We promptly were assigned to some wooden barracks which were to be our homes for about three weeks. After we got settled, the inevitable meeting was called and assignments were handed out. It was decided to run some classes for the combat crews to give them a final brush-up. Because of my armament knowledge, I was put in charge of seeing that the turrets were properly installed, and their guns sighted and harmonized. The airplanes were to be assembled by the Hawaiian Air Depot, which was located on the field.

I had been dissatisfied for some time with our inferior waist and tunnel (tail) armament. There was one gun for all three positions, a ridiculous but typical decision made by brass hats who run our Army. Once at Wright Field, I asked the chief of the armament section why we only had one gun to cover three gun positions. His answer was, "Well, you normally fly in V formation, don't you? Well, the right wing man puts his gun out the right side – left on the left and the leader puts his gun in the tunnel position." If all our top brains were as smart as that guy we'd probably be still flying fabric Keystone bombers.

Anyway, I got a hold of the Air Force Armament Officer, and told him we had to have another 30 and a 50. My idea was to put one 30 out of each side waist window and the 50 out of the tail. He thought that would be fine but he didn't believe that the tail mounts would hold the 50, being designed for a 30. I thought it would and finally fired a 50 round burst from that position with a 50 and he was finally convinced. I could get all the guns I wanted but, the adapters were something else. We have the peculiar custom of letting ordnance supply the guns itself and we furnish everything else, i.e. the recoil adapter, the sockets, sights, cartridge boxes and fasteners, yokes, etc. I thoroughly ransacked all of the Hickam Air Corps warehouses and finally managed to scrape up about 3 good recoil adapters, 7 old style ones, sights and yokes and about an equal amount of 30 caliber stuff. And they called themselves Air Corps supply! Ridiculous! They barely had enough parts to equip ten 50 cal guns and ten 30 cal guns. And they hadn't even requisitioned more from the U.S., we learned later they didn't have a helluva of a lot there. Well, I shot some wires back to the U.S., for about 100 sets and then proceeded to install those 10 sets I had on the first 10 B-26s that were being reassembled. The job was being done by Col. Gilkey's Hawaiian Air Depot. Although his engineering people had never seen a B-26 before, he refused to let our experienced mechanics get in and show them how to put them together and insisted that his civilian mechanics do the whole thing.

As a result we were delayed nearly a month because of their lack of knowledge. Reassembling an airplane has a steep learning curve. ***Editor's note:*** *We have the record of an accident which may have been caused by an improperly installed exhaust manifold.* On 25 February 1942 Chief Depot Engineering Officer, Lt. Col. Albert C. Boyd, on a test flight during takeoff, the right engine burst into flame and ditched into the sea off Fort Kamahaha and ran up onto the mud flats and beach. There were no casualties and the wreck was eventually salvaged. Scratch one sorely needed medium bomber. Ironically this airplane, 40 – 1397, was assigned to 1st Lt. James P. Muri. God we were sore! 1st Lt. Allen continues his narrative:

"He turned my airplane over to me with a severely bent engine mount that probably would have given way on even a slightly hard landing. Our boys picked up the flaw in the first 15 minutes we had the ship. It finally got so that we wouldn't even start the engines of the ships Gilkey turned over until our mechanics gave the ship about a week's inspection and practically rebuilt them from stuff they found wrong. We let them know about it in no uncertain terms but by then he was completely frightened by the airplanes and was of no help at all. He was the most stubborn man I ever met. He painted our rudders with big red and white stripes, making the airplane stand out like a barber pole. As we were getting reports from Java how the Japs were giving grounded airplanes hell with their fighters we naturally didn't want that damn barber pole effect. All our griping had no effect, and they all came out painted that way. The first thing we did when we hit Australia was repaint our tails with camouflage paint. I don't think any one man was ever so hated by the 22nd Bomb Group as that man was.

Well, after delay, after delay, (The Martin B-26 was never intended to be taken apart, I'm convinced), we finally got 'em together, got the guns to fire, calibrated our instruments and were about ready, or at least the 19nd Squadron was ready. At the last minute, however, some damn general somewhere got the idea that there was nothing but Dutch aromatic gasoline where we were going, and as that type of fuel would be dangerous to our rubber gas tanks they had to go back to the Depot and be painted with preservative – another week's delay. During that delay, however, I decided to look around the island, my first visit to Pearl Harbor.

What a sight that was. Six battleships completely under water with only their masts sticking out, and another one, the Nevada, had just been raised and had tremendous holes all through it. There were burned out destroyers, tenders, etc., all over the place. I often wonder when the American public will ever be told of what actually happened that morning. They claim only the Utah and the Arizona were lost. Hell, the rest of those battleships were sunk just like the Arizona. The Nevada was the least damaged, and there was at least a year of work to be done on her. The Japs certainly aren't being fooled. Thousands must have died that morning. Two or three were rolled over on their sides, which must have trapped all inside. The bodies were still in most of them. Never have I ever seen a more devastating job of bombing; my admiration for the planning and technical side of the attack is stupendous.

I wonder if we can approximate their secret planning. By the time the Army and the Navy get through wrangling about who was going to do what, the enemy would know all about it. Visiting some of the other fields I saw some of my old classmates who were now squadron commanders in heavy bombardment and pursuit units. They all thought I was nuts because I like flying a B-26. Well, I figured they could have their "Mack Truck" bombers and out of date pursuit planes if they wanted 'em. I was flying something new. I guess they secretly envied me. I don't know. Everywhere I go when a group of pilots find out I fly a B-26 they ask, "How do you like it?" I tell 'em, "It's the best airplane any Army ever had!" They think I'm nuts. Well at least we don't get shot down – too often.

I went into Honolulu a couple of times and stayed one night at the Royal Hawaiian hotel which had been taken over by the Navy for a rest camp for combat weary aviators and submariners. Of the two, I think the submariners need it the most. They have a helluva life on those damn things. A submarine has no friends and is just as likely to be bombed by friendly ships as by the enemy. Oh well, I ran into quite a few naval aviators who had just returned from raiding the Marshall Islands. It was from them that I got my first clue as to just how really good a Japanese Zero was. They had been flying Grumman F4Fs which is, I believe, our finest Navy fighter even though it can't climb or out-maneuver a Zero. They said they had no trouble attacking their bombers. I'm convinced that as far as pursuit is concerned the F4Fs' superiority is its .50cal guns and above all the men flying them. With an occasional exception Japanese pursuit pilots weren't disciplined. Their bomber pilots, however, appear to be exceptional. Many times I have seen them in perfect formation making a long run despite our ack ack fire and that takes guts.

Well, I'm getting side tracked again. I tell it like it is. One thing I forget to mention was that when we first arrived in Hawaii there was a strict prohibition in effect. I do mean strict! Liquor was definitely not to be had. All the regular boys at Hickam were brewing horrible concoctions made of pineapple juice, raisins and yeast and called "pineapple swipe." One enterprising Lt. who was a flight commander of some B-17s had purchased a small glass still somewhere and he ran it all day on his kitchen stove using pineapple swipe for mash. If carefully watched, by nightfall he had enough alcohol for a party. Nurses were very much in demand, not only because of the shortage of women in Honolulu, but because sometimes they were known to appropriate a little grain alcohol from the hospital. I brought a couple of quarts scotch over from San Francisco and a classmate of mine living at Hickam and I took good care of that. Perhaps the most popular were Navy torpedo men. A torpedo comes equipped with about 15 gallons extra of pure grain alcohol. However, at that time I wasn't fraternally accepted with that Navy crew to have "trading privileges ". Besides after combating officials all day searching for airplane parts I was weary and ready for bed soon after supper.

About the main high spots of my stay in Hawaii were three long distance telephone calls to Jeanne who was staying with my parents in Los Angeles. Despite difficulties with over eager telephone callers and rather poor connections, it was wonderful to hear her voice again. I never could think of anything intelligent to say except that I loved and missed her like anything. Wars wouldn't be nearly so bad if you could have someone you loved with you. In fact, I haven't minded fighting this war so far at all; in fact the challenges were rather fun, but the real hellish part comes from being away from Jeanne.

Editor's note: As 1st Lt. Allen faces the reality of operational flying let's review the training he and other pilots of the 22nd Bombardment Group experienced while checking out in a "hot" airplane, the B-26. **Appendix C**

Chapter Seven

Island Hopping – South Pacific

Well, finally we got down to what we were afraid was coming. In fact we knew it but didn't like to think about it too much. We were to fly to Australia from Hawaii, A-Flight to go first. Warner had been relieved as CO for some reason we never knew and Joe Reed, a former observation pilot who had recently come into the group, took over as he had about four years seniority of service. Walt Mainsberger flew and Joe merely rode as co-pilot. I attended the same briefings as they did, although I really couldn't get it through my mind that I was really going to fly across the Pacific in a medium bomber with a full combat crew, ammunition, a ton of baggage and no extra gasoline. My navigator, my new one that is, was fresh out of navigation school. Reed had grabbed off Wright, my regular navigator. It later turned out well, fortunately, because Wright got badly lost looking for – Canton Airport – and they just got in with only about 10 minutes of gas.

In the briefings, our route, frequencies, descriptions of the landing fields and a lot of hokum about a radio net to give us weather were presented. I still hadn't got a decent compass swing because of the unusually rough air and Tex's inexperience in taking celestial readings on our sun shadow. Finally one morning A-Flight left, leaving Greer, who couldn't get off. I was due to go the following morning. We worried all day about A-Flight and finally that afternoon we got word that they had landed safely at Palmyra Atoll about 1,300 miles south of the Hawaiian islands. Then we started worrying about ourselves. I was to have five ships in my flight: Myself, Larson, Cooper, Bumgarner and Greer – who was supposed to have left with A-Flight. That afternoon I picked up a Springfield rifle from ordnance. That was to be our ground defense when we got to Australia. I decided that I ought to have a Browning Automatic Rifle (BAR), so that evening I gave the Ordnance officer a few drinks, and he got me one. I still have it.

Our baggage, we had decided, was to be limited to 40 pounds. I had 75 pounds but some of the crew had less so I figured it would be OK. When we weighed Tex's it came to 120 pounds. He claimed he had all his navigation equipment packed so I didn't argue. It turned out later he had a case and a half of Canadian Club. Came in handy, too. At the last minute they ran two passengers in on me and on each of the other ships. Mine was a Major in the Signal Corps who had been a former Bell executive in New York. Helluva good guy, but still another 200 pounds. Well, about midnight I finally turned in after taking a final check on the weather. It didn't look too hot, but being the eternal optimist I figured it would clear up. I hoped. I had no sooner hit the bed when someone was waking me up. "Wake up, Chief. It's time to go." "Go? Go where?! Go away; I'm sleepy." "Look chum, you've got to fly across the ocean. Remember?" With sort of a sinking feeling I rolled out of bed, hopped on a truck along with the other crews, made a final check on the weather on the way down to the flying line, and still half asleep stood around by my plane waiting for the final word to go. Haskins came up and gave me sort of a hail and farewell handshake and a brief pep talk along the lines of, "Allen, I don't have to worry about you. I know you'll get your flight to Australia," etc.

Finally, 17 March 1942, around five, I got the go signal, so I started up, taxied down to the end of the runway and took off. I told the rest of the flight I would make one circle of the field and then get on course, which I did. As it was dark I didn't see any of the others immediately. About an hour out I picked up Greer, Cooper and Bumgarner. I learned a little later that Larson got off a little late, got nearly half way to Palmyra on his own when his fuel transfer pump went out. He returned to Hawaii, landed at Hickam with about five gallons of gas.

Our plan to fly abreast with about three miles separation so we would cover quite a wide front and also be separated enough to prevent danger of running into each other in case of weather. About 30 minutes out of Hawaii we ran into a first class tropical front and for nearly an hour I found myself at sea level, flying instruments through heavy rain and of course unable to contact any of the other ships. I was unable to take any drift readings. "A fine way to start" I thought. After a while, I began to get worried for I knew we had probably flown through several wind shifts which we had been unable to record. Finally the weather broke and was OK the rest of the way to Palmyra. The only trouble was that we had been blown off course about 20 miles to the right and didn't know it. Fortunately there is a small reef about 20 miles to the right (west) of Palmyra and we intercepted that and were able to go right on in without any undue searching.

Palmyra is a reef about four miles long and about a mile wide with a lot of palm trees on it. When we landed about one PM, it was hotter than hell. All the ships seemed to be OK, so we refueled and grabbed a bite to eat. I had a helluva argument with a testy old Navy Captain who said, "I'm King of this island and you will do as I say," but we took off anyway, for Canton Island Airport about 1,000 miles away. The weather forecast was fair, and I asked Palmyra to ask Canton to give me a weather forecast when we were half way there, but they never did. On the way to Palmyra, from position reports from other ships, I had become convinced that our compass had a minus 3 degree error in the vicinity of reading 220 degrees. Tex didn't think so, but as I have done quite a lot of D.R. (Dead

Reckoning) navigation and I learned always to respect a hunch, I set in +3 degrees of "Kentucky windage." Thank God I did. Somehow Tex got his ground speed gummed up and about 30 minutes before my computation of our expected arrival, Tex announced that unless we flew due south, (a 30 degree course change) we were going to miss the damn place. It was a hard decision to make but my hunches have always worked so far, so I continued on course. Tex promptly checked his notes and I think his rescue gear as well. Sure enough in about 30 minutes Canton Island showed up. I've never been so relieved. Especially as there were only about 30 minutes of daylight left. Canton is almost impossible to find in the daytime, let alone at night, so we were fortunate. Canton is a coral reef shaped something like a pork chop with a lagoon in the middle. It is about five miles long and about two miles wide and for vegetation has one sparse palm tree which is probably phony. How anything can live on that damn island I don't know. Oh, yes. On the way to Canton we crossed the equator, but as our navigator at the time was a little uncertain, we weren't overly excited about becoming shell backs or whatever the air equivalent is.

At Canton we caught up with A-Flight although I never did see them there. We RON (Remain Over Night). There were about 1,000 troops which had arrived a few weeks before at the island. Their ship ran aground at the entrance to the lagoon and they were a pretty miserable bunch. All the drinking water was contaminated with oil, and all their equipment was that as well. 500 Japs could have taken Canton if they had known. The Japanese-held Marshall Islands were only a few hundred miles north. I and crew and our two passengers went around to their camp for something to eat. We discovered they had some cold beer. As it was 120 degree in the shade, but no shade, after about two cans I didn't care if we ever got to Australia. I couldn't find anyone on the island of any authority except a corporal manning the Pan Am radio station on the runway. There were tents over by the airplanes and after playing with the hermit crabs for a while I turned in. The place was infested with monstrous rats which kept us awake most of the night. The next morning, after a brief visit to the weather station we took off again.

Although that was our longest hop, on 18 March 1942, some 1,400 miles, it was one of our easiest as the Fiji Islands are pretty large and the weather was fairly good for a change. We arrived at the little New Zealand Air Force field at Nandi early in the afternoon, where we again ran into A-Flight. After refueling we went to the RNZ Officer Mess and drank a couple of New Zealand beers. Their beer is like our ale and it only took a couple to make a Christian out of you. Reed was sore because I didn't contact him in Canton but as far as I was concerned I was running my own show until we got to Australia. Reed in my mind was still an observation pilot, (he rarely flew as 1st pilot in a B-26 as he didn't like them much). I was never able to acquire a great deal of respect for him.

Nearly all of us had airplane trouble in Fiji. I had a short in my prop relay circuit; Cooper's fuel booster pump had gone out; Chris Herron of A-Flight had torn the valve stem out of one of his main gear tires. So A-Flight went on to New Caledonia without him and I stayed an extra day with Cooper, Herron and Bumgarner. Geer went on with A-Flight. Herron rigged up a makeshift valve stem, and we got some prop parts from a P-39. They were 24-volt parts and didn't work, although we eliminated the short.

We, RON and had time so we drove into Nandi, a small town of around 2,000, mostly native, and sent Jeanne a post card. We also stopped in at a native village where we were received as visiting royalty. The Fiji natives are about the finest I've ever seen. The women are ugly but the men are very muscular and handsome, and all of them are amazingly clean. They are all exceptionally good natured, and constantly greet you with cries of "Bula" which is sort of a universal word meaning hello, good-by, how are you, I'm fine and what have you. I gave the King some cigarettes which he promptly gave to the other natives. He and his wife were the only ones who could speak any kind of English. They took us all over the village and into a good number of native homes. Their houses are all made of grass and for floors they have several thick grass mats all spotlessly clean. They have no furniture, that is, all but the King's home which actually had a throne for the King and Queen. The Queen, I think, ran the show in the village for she gave most of the orders and did most of the talking. I liked the Fiji natives tremendously. The other natives of the islands were descendants of low caste Indians imported by the British from India years ago. They were a poor type, surly, dirty and in general pretty crude. At that, however, the Fiji natives were, or had been, cannibals. Indecently, they all wore sarongs – male and female – their feet are tremendously wide. Exactly like a duck's.

The army representative at Nandi was an Air Corps colonel who had gone British. That is, he had a big mustache, wore a big sun helmet, even spoke with a British accent and palled around with the New Zealanders who seemed to tolerate him and resent our landing at their airfield. The colonel said, "When we reached New Caledonia we weren't supposed to land at Noumea, but instead go up the coast another 75 miles and land at a new airport, Plaines de Gaiacs," he assured us it had been completed and had full facilities. For that misinformation alone I could have gladly shot him. Besides he wasn't going to let Herron take off because of his tire. I told Chris that if he figured it was OK, to start up with me and in-as-much as Cooper was going to have to stay, the Colonel would think Chris was Cooper and vice versa. In the morning, however, Cooper was still struggling with his fuel pump. They were trying to start it by pouring raw gasoline into the carburetor air intakes. Actually the engine started a few times but died just before the engine pump was about to draw gasoline into the carburetor. It was pretty disheartening work, so we finally had to take off without him.

Our next stop was New Caledonia on 19 March 1942. I originally planned to stop in New Caledonia just long enough to refuel and then go right on to Brisbane, but I hadn't reckoned with New

Caledonian inadequate air services. The weather was fairly good the first half of the trip but about 100 miles from New Caledonia the ceiling went down to a few hundred feet with pretty heavy rain We did pass right over the southern tip of Mare Island, a small island about 70 miles from New Caledonia. That gave us an excellent fix. I was afraid that the weather might get worse and possibly we might run right into New Caledonian mountains while on instruments, so I steered slightly south so we would come into the southern tip of the island. The weather remained about the same and soon we were coming into Noumea Harbor exchanging recognition signals with a bunch of destroyers and cruisers in the harbor. Noumea airport, La Tontouta, we were instructed not to land there so we flew up the coast and finally found the field, Plaines des Gaiacs, about 70 miles up the coast. Circling the field I saw A-Flight up at one end of it and I wondered why they were still up there. I soon found out. As soon as I hit the ground I realized I had made a mistake. The damn field wasn't finished yet. Instead of being a hard landing strip as it had appeared from the air it was a sea of mud. I slithered down to the end of it where my right wheel promptly sunk down in the mud a couple of feet. Hell! Chris came in OK and then Bumgarner landed. He blew his left tire as he hit and damn near wound up in a swamp alongside the strip. By a damn good piece of work he managed to straighten out and he finally stopped, only to sink down in the runway.

A-Flight had been there over night and had finally gotten unstuck. There was no gasoline. Fortunately the French contractors building the field had a cat and a lot of natives. After working hard all afternoon we got Bumgarner's ship off the runway after having dug one wheel out of the mud that was so deep that the left wing tip was within a foot of the ground. Hours later we managed to take off from Plaines des Gaiacs. A-Flight, Herron and I from B-Flight flew down to La Tontouta where we should have landed in the first place. We blessed that damn Colonel and his misinformation at Fiji! As Major Gregory, one of my passengers put it in his poem, "Some

New Zealand boot, which a father doth lack, sent us by air to the Plaines des Gaiacs!"

La Tontouta is a new airfield; about 40 miles by road from Noumea, pretty good although servicing facilities consisted of hand pumps cranked by some islanders who were so enthused that they nearly wore out the pumps. The mosquitoes were unusually voracious, so I commandeered a 2 ½ ton G.I. truck, loaded the passengers on it and was about to start into Noumea to wire Hickam not to let anyone go to Plaines des Gaiacs in the future and also have the next flight bring a tire for Bumgarner and a pump for Cooper. As we were starting out, however, Greer came rushing up and announced his passenger, Colonel Collins of the Army was dying and we must rush him to the hospital in Noumea at once. The colonel, a 250 pound old-time Army Colonel who wasn't enjoying the flight much anyway, apparently was dying as we lifted him up in the cab of the truck, and off we went on the 40 mile ride through the mountains to the Free French city of Noumea. I thoughtfully brought along a bottle of Canadian Club which I had been saving for just such an emergency.

There was Jack Lee, Mike Shea, Commander Metcalf, a Lend Lease guy from Washington named Digby, and myself, and oh yes, Colonel Collins dying in the front seat. As tired and as hot as we were, despite our number the Canadian Club cheered us up no end, and during the ride we made up a humorous poem about our trip which at the time seemed about the funniest thing we had ever heard. No one was especially concerned about the Colonel and he later commented on it. "There I was dying in the front seat and you guys celebrating my wake in the back end."

When we were nearly to Noumea we ran into the Army major who loaned us the truck. One of his tanks had driven off the road, and the narrow road was blocked and apparently would be for some time. It seems that the truck we borrowed was the major's ammunition truck, and he was sore as hell about it. In as much as I had been running the show so far, I was sort-of-shoved up to do the talking. I talked fast and furiously for a few minutes, and I guess the spectacle of a 1st Lt. giving a major hell was too much; he slowly shook his head, pointed to his command car on the other side of the blocked road and said, "Son, take it and get going." Now, thinking about it the more amazing it gets. Here I was with a full colonel, a Navy commander, two majors, a captain and a Washington man under my wing, so to speak, telling off a rather surprised Infantry major who probably ranked with God in his own bailiwick. Anyway, we finally got to Noumea. I got off at headquarters to send my messages, and the rest went on to the hospital with the colonel.

The Army CO of New Caledonia was pretty swell. I sent my messages without any trouble, and then he gathered around his staff and had me tell about the trip, etc. They had just gotten there themselves apparently. Later I went on over to the hospital where the chief nurse took charge and assigned us attendants who made sure we showered and shaved and then promptly put us to bed. What a lucky break! The rest of the gang, back at the field, didn't make out too well and were badly bitten by mosquitoes. The next morning, 20 March 1942, I picked up the weather report and got a truck to get us back to Tontouta. The colonel, it seems, wasn't dying after all but merely had acute indigestion caused by his eating two steaks for breakfast in Fiji.

Chapter Eight

Australia – Red Tape

So at nearly noon we started off again, 20 March 1942 – with what were left of A and B-Flights – after a rather uneventful flight we reached the Australian coast. Herron had strayed off to the right about 50 miles so I circled around the coast waiting for him while the rest went on into Brisbane. I had hoped to land first. Herron showed up and we landed at Archer Field. It was grass and only about 3,000 feet long. A lousy field in general but what a relief to get the ocean flight over with.

After getting the men a place to stay we made a beeline for the Lemons Hotel, a favorite watering hole according to the men at the field. We took a street car called a tram and were somewhat amazed to find everything about the same as in the states, except everyone drove on the wrong side of the road. The Lemons was an extremely good hotel and we all got big suites equipped with a lot of overstuffed chairs and radios. Colonel Collins, my passenger, was the hero of the whole affair. We no sooner arrived when he threw a big party for us. I never saw a guy so happy to arrive in a place as he was. He started ordering up cases of Scotch and food. It turned out, as you can guess, quite a party. It was a relief to sit in a big comfortable chair in an air-conditioned hotel room and just relax. Nothing to worry about. Joe Reed was now running the show and I had absolutely nothing to do.

We arrived in Brisbane March 20, 1942. After three days in

Brisbane we were ordered up to Townsville where we were based at Garbutt Field. I was there only one night when I heard Larson had landed hard at Archer, had skidded on the wet grass and hit a Dutch B-25 parked on the field, so I flew back down to survey the damage and see what the score was. Colonel Haskins came in the next day, and I flew back to Townsville with Larson's crew as passengers.

I no sooner got back to Townsville when Haskins wired that General Brett, down in Melbourne wanted two B-26s and crews to start finding out how to drop torpedoes and for me to grab someone in my Flight and go down to Melbourne pronto to see what it was all about. Bumgarner had damaged a wing in Townsville and Larson's ship had a smashed nose, so I grabbed onto Cooper, and away we went, 27 March 1942, to Brisbane.

Our next stop, after leaving Brisbane, was Sydney, Australia's largest city. For navigation I had a couple of Australian land maps and a Shell road map which turned out to be accurate and the most helpful. I decided to land at Bankstown, the RAAF airdrome near Sydney but after landing I promptly got stuck. Fortunately, Cooper hadn't landed yet so I called him on the radio and told him to go over to Mascot, the municipal airport, as Bankstown was too muddy. After about an hour of digging we finally got the ship out of the mud. As I was surveying the field trying to figure out a way to take off, an RAAF officer came running out and said Cooper was phoning me. I picked up the phone in the control tower and this was the conversation – it was Cooper, "Chief?" "Yes." "I've got some bad news for you." (I thought, Christ, now what?) "Well?" "One of my landing gears collapsed." I thought Holy smoke! That meant a total washout. I managed to take off and land over at Mascot – a very short field – sure enough there was Coop's ship down on one wing. The fuselage was buckled so there went, one each, another B-26. Coop was standing around looking foolish as hell. I parked and asked, "What happened?" Coop was up front and honest. "I reached for the flap handle to take up the flaps after landing but grabbed the wheel handle by mistake."

A $250,000 airplane lost because of error. So many things had already happened that I couldn't even get mad. What I was mainly concerned about was how I was going to explain this to the general. I wired him, one airplane had washed out because of landing gear failure (which was partially true) and wired Col Haskins to see if I couldn't get another one. I left Cooper with instructions to go back to Brisbane with enough salvaged parts to put Larson's ship back in service at Archer Field where he had skidded into the parked B-25.

The trip over to Melbourne was a new revelation. We had a dandy map – for a change. I noticed that the highest mountain on the course was marked 2,700. The weather was bad and at about 5,000 I went on instruments. I flew for about 20 minutes and when there was a small break I noticed mountains on all sides, and higher than I was. I grabbed for altitude as fast as 'ole 1498 would climb and broke out on top at 13,000 feet. I then rechecked the map and discovered the damn thing was marked "International" and elevations were in meters. Not feet! Although a bit late, it was an important discovery. The weather at Melbourne was lousy and having never been there before I had a helluva time getting in. I landed at Laverton, 30 miles from Melbourne, in a heavy rainstorm, which is no fun in a B-26 as the curved windshield goes opaque in the rain. I arrived jerkily, looking out the side window, just missing a line of B-17s. After considerable delay I finally got a ride to headquarters to report. I couldn't find anyone with authority and finally was turned over to Colonel Eubanks who was then Ass't. Chief of Staff or something. He had been the CO of the 19th Group in Java and the Philippines. He seemed to know all about the whole thing and promptly found a fairly young major on his staff who, Colonel Eubanks said, would take charge of the project. He talked pretty big. *(**Editor's note:** It had not yet been fully explained but a project was afoot to find out if a B-26 could carry and effectively drop a torpedo.)* Meanwhile time was a-wasting with useless activity eventually there will be established a torpedo training facility at Nowra near Jervis Bay, 125 miles south of Sydney. We went across the street to RAAF headquarters to see what they knew about the project. We got hold of a rather gloomy squadron leader who was full of talk about a big RAAF torpedo training school to be set up in a few months. Our major seemed impressed. We then went to the U.S. Navy headquarters. Their staff knew nothing about a torpedo school.

I tagged along listening to a lot of talk about what was going to be done "in the future." I was beginning to get discouraged. On the second day I happened to run into Dick Carlisle, a classmate of mine who flew a B-17 in combat in Java. He clued me in on front-line opinions. He said that MacArthur was not liked by anyone who had been in the Philippines or Java; that Colonel Eubanks had cost the 19th Bombardment Group most of its airplanes by foolishly having them parked in neat rows in the Philippines. About the major I had been running around with, who talked about Zeros and combat, Dick said, "He hadn't been on a single mission."

Everyone I met had just come down from Java and had been in the Philippines before that. All were sore as hell about the generalship and MacArthur and Eubanks seemed to get all the blame. This was quite a surprise to me because I had assumed from all the publicity that MacArthur was a hero. My closest contact to him came one day when I was out at the field and a full colonel and a major came up and announced that they were on MacArthur's air staff and had been sent out to find out all about the B-26, and that I was to check the major out in the ship. I told them that if they wanted to be checked out they would first have to have written permission from my group commander (knowing full well he wouldn't approve unless ordered to) and that he would have to have 30 hours of dual instruction. It worked. I had 'em there. To soften their disappointment I said I'd take 'em up. The major flew as copilot. After I got up around 7,000 I let him take over. He did and suddenly slapped on full right rudder,

completely stalling us out. We damn near went into a spin. I took the controls away from him and went down and landed. Major or no major, I was sore as hell. He later, still a bit white, said he wanted to see how it would do a bomb run. I never heard anything so foolish. There was a 40 mile an hour cross wind when I landed and the field, being messed up, caused the landing to be fast and rough. The colonel and the major both turned white when I greased it in. As soon as I parked they left and I wasn't bothered by them again. . I began to think, however, that if they were a sample of MacArthur or his staff someone's surly getting fooled.

Chapter Nine

Perth – Torpedo Testing

After about a week of this foolishness, the break finally came. Little General George, the pursuit man, and apparently the only one around who wasn't a blow hard or stuffed shirt, called for me. He said, and not very kindly, "You've been messing around for a week and nothing has been accomplished." He thought apparently I was the only one around the place that knew anything about torpedoes or the B-26; that I was now in full charge of finding out whether or not a B-26 could drop torpedoes and, if so, how; and that as long as I got results I could do anything I like, and he would back me up. And he didn't waste word one telling me. It was a terrible loss to the Corps when he was killed about two months later in Darwin (29 April 1942) by one of his own P-40s. (*Editor's note*: *Brig. Gen. Harold H. "Pursuit" George was struck on the ground by accident when a P-40 lost directional control while taking off at Batchelor Field, SE of Darwin.*)

I decided that I would go to Perth where they had some torpedoes and learn how to drop 'em. So I did. I arrived around the first of May at Pearce Airdrome, about 30 miles from Perth, Western Australia. It was quite a thrill to see the Indian Ocean for the first time. It made me realize I was actually on the other side of the world; India and continental Africa was just an ocean away. The first thing I did after getting quarters on the field for the crew was to run into navy headquarters in town. I told the chief of staff my story, and he

promptly assigned Commander Robinson (Robie) to work with me. The commander knew nothing about airplanes but a helluva lot about torpedoes, and the whole idea intrigued him immensely. Robinson was a man, all business with tremendous drive. His manner gave one the impression he was angry at everything and everybody – including you. It took me a while to recognize it was his way – his personality.

The first step was to build a dummy torpedo with which to make the initial drops. This turned out to be quite a problem. There wasn't a factory available with facilities for making a steel one. The RAAF suggested we make one of Jarrah wood. Jarrah is a tree native to Western Australia and its wood is like iron and nearly as heavy. So we got the largest company of wood workers in town to make one for us. Robinson did a swell job there. The local wood workers were quite a trial. The workmen on the dummy nearly drove Commander Robinson and me crazy. They would start work at 9:00, knock off at 10:30 for tea, and back at 11:00, then off to lunch at 1:00, back at 2:00, tea again at 4:00 and then home at 5:30. We fumed and complained, "You're holding up the war." But you can't hurry a West Australian. In their defense I will say the Perthians are by far the nicest and friendliest of the Australians. It took nearly a month to complete making a wood torpedo. In the meantime there wasn't a thing for us to do but sit around the RAAF station and enjoy life.

Pearce Airdrome is Australia's best equipped field – having large brick buildings and an officer's mess that would do credit to any of our army fields in the U.S. During that time we got to know the Australian pilots very well. I have never met a finer bunch. Beer was plentiful, and the Aussies were curious about us and vice versa. Our favorite sport was arguing. The average Aussie is more quiet and reserved than we are, but that doesn't last long. We debated about everything under the sun. British planes vs. ours – small railroad box cars vs. U.S. box cars. Aussies compared to the English, etc. One night we'd argue for American things, and the next night we'd switch sides like a regular Oxford debating society lubricated by quantities of beer.

We were rather at a disadvantage. For example, I'd start arguing with some pilots from Number 14 Squadron and after about 10 beers, Number 77 Squadron, still fresh would reinforce them, and about two in the morning or so, Number 20 Squadron would pitch in. On the whole we could out-drink them ten to one. Although we didn't discover that for some time. The squadron leaders would generally work on me first. The arrival of Cooper was a blessing – debating-drinking reinforcements at last!

After a couple of weeks the Aussies began to wonder if our B-26 would actually fly, in as much as I hadn't budged it since I arrived. I had no spare parts and you can't fly any airplane without them. After Cooper arrived, Thompson, Coop's copilot, and Willy got restless not flying, and it was quite a problem keeping them under control. All of 77th Squadron, which had new P-40s and were pleased as punch about them, were just waiting for the day we would fly to see if we could really go as fast as we alleged.

Finally the great day arrived. Commander Robinson's wood torpedo and torpedo carrier arrived. We planned the torpedo drop in great detail. Using detailed admiralty charts of the Swan River, we decided to the exact foot where his "baby" was to be dropped. We had a crash boat loaded with divers and gear. This torpedo would not float. A radio frequency was selected so that any last minute changes could be flashed to me. The head of the Newport Naval Station had arrived for the occasion. The admiral was to be here. The RAAF Air Commander was to be there. All in all, a gala affair – planned and timed to be executed with true Navy efficiency.

Only one thing was overlooked. The eccentricities of a flying machine. We tested the dropping gear with a secondary dummy. The real dummy was installed – I shook hands with everyone – all the RAAF was out to watch the takeoff. My plan was to make a takeoff and a landing with the damn thing on to see if it could be done first, and then fly over to Perth and drop it at 200 mph at 200 feet. Well, we got in the ship and I tried to start the engines. Surprise! Surprise! Both booster coils on the right and left engine burned out in succession. I hadn't burned out booster coils in months, and this day both of them burned out. No way can you start a 2,000 horsepower engine without a booster coil.

I was sure we didn't have any spares but Sgt. Harrum, my crew chief, with characteristic ability for saving the day when all seems lost, came through and dug up two spares. Robinson ran and I phoned the Perth crew that we would be late while the coils were being changed. I paced back and forth. In a few minutes the coils were changed and once again I tried to start up. This time the batteries were dead. Both had "boiled over" on the flight across the Pacific and now, after nearly a month of inactivity, they chose this, of all times, to fail. The ground crew wasn't to be daunted. Holden and Harrum got out the hand crank and cranked the big internal inertia starter by hand. After two tries the right engine started, and I got the left one going from the generator of the other. At last! I checked the engines and taxied out.

About half way out to the end of the field Sgt. Harrum came up between the two seats and announced that the torpedo had just fallen off! I thought what next? I turned around and sure enough it was lying on the ground about a hundred yards from where we loaded it. By now it was noon and we were supposed to have dropped the "thing" at 10:00. I taxied back to the line and shut the motors off and got out. Robinson looked very unhappy, and I guess I was no ray of sunshine. Well, we decided to try it after lunch if I could find out why the damn thing released. It would have been a helluva note if we accidently dropped it when flying over the city. A 2,000 pound dead weight going 200 mph, perish the thought!

I sent the crew out to bring back lunch while I started working on the release gear. After about an hour's work, I finally discovered the firing switch had a short in it, and the release gear was improperly adjusted so that the gear was in the "armed" position when it was supposedly "safe." About 1:30 we were ready to go again. I took off, flew around the field, landed and then took off again with Cooper flying alongside to watch. I made two practice passes and then dropped the "thing "on the third run. After I got back to the field I jumped in a car and drove into town to find out what had happened. Plenty! It turned out. The "thing" had hit the water, bounced, done a couple of summersaults and reentered the water – backwards! A real torpedo would have broken up under the stress. A standard aerial torpedo is designed to be dropped by a slow flying airplane at around 100 knots. We were using twice that speed.

After a two day search for our "torpedo" the divers finally gave up. The bottom of the Swan River was ten feet of gooey mud, something we hadn't counted on. So after all the preparation we had lost our "torpedo which had taken so long to build (costing 500 Aus. Pounds – about 1,700 dollars.), and all we knew was one way not to drop a torpedo. It took a long time before we ever learned all the causes for that first failure. Well – I had visions of General George fuming over my dispatches. But he never said a word one way or another. We ordered three more dummies. The workmen now had the knack of making these and the first of the new order was ready in 10 days. We decided to make our next drops slower at 180 mph and at 180 feet and then increasing the altitude until we got a combination of an entrance angle into the water that prevented the Torpedo from bouncing out again and still not dive too deep.

We made movies of each drop and then developed them that night in Commander Robinson's bath tub in his hotel room in Perth. The film came out in negative form, but that didn't matter because we could stop the projector on any frame and measure the angle of entrance into the water. After about 10 dummy drops we decided to drop a live torpedo with an exercise head which is filled with water. At the end of the torpedo run, compressed air drives the water from the head and the torpedo floats to the surface ready for another exercise. We decided to drop it at 180 mph and from 220 feet. The torpedo dropped OK and that was the last anyone saw it until the following day when divers recovered the pieces. A $10,000 "fish" ruined, but we knew why. The damn head had collapsed from the shock, catapulting it and breaking it in half. We got a foundry busy making a reinforced head for the next drop. We made some more dummy drops at higher speeds. During these tests both Coop and I were carrying various RAAF officers and enlisted men along with us for the ride. Squadron Leader Graham, then CO of 14 Squadron, complained that I was ruining the morale of his boys by taking them with us. They flew slow Lockheed Hudsons.

When a torpedo is placed under the belly of a B-26 the mounting connector is called a "saddle"; here a bombardier and a ground-crew member "ride" bareback, rodeo style, on an unsaddled practice torpedo.

A 2,000 pound practice navy torpedo at Nowra, New South Wales. Note: When under-slung on a B-26 the torpedo clearance is only 4 inches above the PSP – Pierced Steel Plank "pavement."

"Torpedo Away!" A test drop at Perth, Western Australia.

Chapter Ten

Chasing the Enemy

We had one squabble with the RAAF. A B-26 is extremely sloppy and difficult to handle with the wheels down. And it takes a lot of power to keep it in the air. The RAAF rules at the time were that we were to make a complete circuit of the field with our wheels down. In most ships it doesn't make much difference except in speed. Both Coop and I refused to do this. We both knew that the ack-ack gunners knew us. In fact that was the start of the whole trouble. One night after supper the ack-ack major suggested to me that when Coop and I came back from the next morning's drop we come in low over the field to give his gunners some tracking practice. His battery hadn't had that type of practice since Crete where they held the record of 60 enemy planes shot down.

Well, Coop and I were only too happy to oblige. We came blazing across in close formation around 270 mph just over the tops of the trees, swooped over the hangar line, pulled up into a steep climbing turn and back down on the gun positions again a little below the tops of the hangars. When we landed Wing Commander Heflin met us and was sore as hell. "Violation of Rules!" he said. Well hell, we were just doing a favor for the ack-ack boys, who were pleased as hell about the whole exercise. We consistently refused to do this silly flying around with our wheels down. Wing Commander finally called in Air Commodore De La Rue – a fiery old dragon from the old school to give me hell and see to it that I would damn well obey the traffic rules. The only trouble was that two days earlier something rather significant to sweeten US – Aussie relations had happened.

About nine o'clock in the evening 3 May 1942, Navy operations called me up and told me that a Jap carrier was believed to be in the vicinity of Geraldton, about 200 miles north of Perth, and were my B-26s ready to go? Cooper's was out at the time but mine was ready to go. O.K! Independent of any RAAF action I called Robie and asked him to get me a torpedo and some 500 pound demolition bombs. I had the only airplane in Western Australia capable of carrying anything bigger than a 250 pound bomb. The other airplanes were Lockheed Hudsons and there were only three of them. And, oh yes, the Navy had a few decrepit PBYs that had been all through Java.

Robie had to get a warhead and the bombs from a dump about 40 miles away, get a torpedo charged and brought out. I didn't see how he could do it, but by 2:00 AM they all arrived. That man could get things done quicker than anyone I ever saw. Of course he had been through the Philippines and Java campaigns and knew the score. And how he hated MacArthur! About 3:00 AM the RAAF wanted to know what I was going to do about the whole thing. I told them I was loaded with 1,200 gallons of gas, three 500 pound bombs, a 2,000 pound torpedo and three cases of extra ammunition, and as soon as anyone located the carrier I would do my best to sink it. 77 Squadron had two flights of P-40s ready to go in case the carrier came close!

At dawn, 4 May 1942, I got the order. Proceed in the direction of Geraldton and the location of the carrier would be radioed to me if located. Otherwise, land at Geraldton. Well, I was carrying a gross load of 36,000 pounds which wasn't bad for an airplane designed for a gross of 31,000. Counting my bomb bay tank of extra gas, I was carrying a payload of 6,000 pounds or a bomb load of a fully loaded B-24. *Editor's Note: Martin engineers determined this was the heaviest wing loading ever flown by a Marauder at 88 pounds per square inch.* And Pearce airdrome is 3,500 feet long. Well, I told the crew I thought I could make it but for them this was strictly a voluntary mission. Naturally they all stayed, including Sgt. Harrum and Sgt. Wilson, our torpedo specialist. My plan of attack was to stay down on the water – drop the fish – go like hell for about 100 miles, and then come back at high altitude and drop the bombs, then dive for the water and go like hell for Geraldton and re-bomb with Aussie 500 pound bombs. I carried a couple of cases of shackle adaptors so they would fit.

We were ready. Robie was there. He shook hands with me and away we went. That B-26 took off like it was a B-19. That takeoff convinced me that the B-26 is the finest airplane in the world. I always have known since I first flew it in March of 1941, but this was the payoff. Our initial climb was a little slow, but once we got a little speed away we went as if we were empty. The three Hudsons had taken off about five minutes ahead of me, but we passed those about 15 miles out. We were climbing around 700 feet a minute, and it was as if they were standing still. Old 1498 was a magnificent airplane. Incidentally, I learned only a few days before that Chris Herron, the former owner of 1498, had been killed in a forced landing returning from a mission on Rabaul.

Well, no call from Pearce so we landed at Geraldton. I figured the plane fast, but I underestimated. I glided in under power at 155 and leveled off about five feet off the ground. The ship stalled cold at 135 just before it hit. That's probably as fast a speed as any airplane has ever stalled at. Anyway, the landing was soft and we taxied up in front of operations. We must have been quite a sight. The most modern bomber in the world suddenly arriving in this remote corner of the earth with a live torpedo strapped on its belly. I lined up a supply of 500 pound bombs and refueled. We stood by until 1:00 PM until the Navy wired us that it was all off. The carrier had apparently gone off somewhere and was out of our range. It was then, and then only, I began to realize how lucky I was. Here, a single airplane;

carrying the equivalent load of one torpedo plane and three dive bombers going out alone to sink an enemy carrier. Funny thing, though, I'm just damn fool enough to think we'd have gotten away with it. One other thing, we had damn good gunners. Well, now I had to fly this load home again. The Navy wanted their bombs and torpedo back. So off we went.

On landing at Perth I glided in at 165 and set her down at 145. That was about right. I landed, turned around, and started to taxi when – WHAM! The left tire blew out. Everyone on board nearly had heart failure! All I could do was get the ship stopped; we weren't going very fast. I weakly stuck my head out the window and looked. If that tire had blown a few seconds earlier, I imagined, but thank God I made one of the best landings of my life. Carrying Explosives? It wasn't the TNT we were carrying, it was the air flask of the torpedo, and 1,800 pounds of compressed air would go off with as much violence as a bomb. My fish was clearing the ground by only one inch! Well we were back. We dragged old 1498 back and parked her in front of the hangars.

Well, all of this leads up to Wing Commander Heflin's tiff and a meeting with Air Commodore De La Rue who said if we didn't put our wheels down and fly the pattern they'd tell the ack-ack boys to fire at us. I smiled; I knew we had nothing to fear from our friends the ack-ack boys. Then Dalaroo said with audacity, that we had taken off with that torpedo without his permission. That was the payoff. I told him that I had come over to Perth not to defend the damn place but to do experimental work. I had on my own free will, volunteered to act as a strike force in case anything showed up, and when something did show up, I was the only airplane available to do something about it. And as far as the fish was concerned, I asked if he thought that little 250 pound bombs the Hudsons carried were expected to sink anything? He saw the point and quieted down. After that my relations with the RAAF were most cordial, and a written order came out permitting us to fly as we chose.

Chapter Eleven

Nowra – Operational Training

Well, it finally got to the point where we weren't learning much new. We knew by then a couple of speeds and altitudes that we could guarantee successful torpedo runs, but I was convinced by then that there was plenty more to learn. Robie began to be less help as he began getting academic about the process. I knew damn well in reality with enemy AA fire and Zeros on your tail, no pilot would stick to the close limits we had set up. General George had sent out a colonel to get a full report. He arrived one late afternoon in a transport. I took him over to the club and fed him a couple of quick double scotches – that was a mistake. I took him into town, fed him and then wrote out his report for him. General George sent a note asking if I wanted six more B-26s to make a torpedo squadron. I made a mistake by saying "Not yet. I want to learn a little more first." I had no way of knowing he would be accidentally killed a few weeks later. Well, we dropped another fish in the Swan; it stuck in the mud and was never recovered. At least it didn't break up, which proved our reinforced head was a success.

I wired General Brett, 1 July 1942; I was coming back and was ready to instruct B-26 crews in torpedo launching at the supposedly completed torpedo school at Nowra, 125 miles south of Sydney, near Jervis Bay, New South Wales. I had checked Willy and Thompson out as first pilots, but in a practice landing they broke a down-lock on the nose gear, so I went to Sydney alone. I discovered that Nowra was a long way from being completed. In fact, the RAAF torpedo training program didn't exist. No one knew the score about anything. Our Navy, however, was very interested. Commander Kelly, Navy Chief of Staff, knew what we had done at Perth and gave us Lt. "Fuzzy" Drake, an old time naval airman who knew his torpedoes. Fuzzy was a lucky break. I had our motion pictures taken at Perth, so I got General Brett to see them. The General wasn't particularly interested in torpedoes or apparently much of anything, but General "Hap" Arnold had been sending some pretty hot letters to "get busy," so once again I was "It."

"Fuz" and I got together with an old Navy Warrant Officer, Gunner Andrews, and the three of us prepared an action plan. I decided to fly over to Nowra and look the place over. It seems that some joker had cracked up a B-26 there about a month before and claimed it was due to the field being faulty. So the Air Force gave me an obsolete Dutch Curtis Falcon. After a couple of days delay due to weather, Fuz and I set off. The Falcon would only go about an hour and a half on a tank of gas, so we landed all over southeastern Australia refueling. The little thing looked like a Zero and I think we would have been shot down at some RAAF fields if they had any ack-ack guns. All the instruments were metric, so I didn't know what I was doing. The only thing I could read was the tachometer and the clock. Nowra turned out to be a mile-long strip with a few RAAF shacks they called billets. A couple of RAAF boys were in charge – Wing Commander Walker and Squadron Leader Gadd. They didn't know much about the set-up either, but there were facilities suitable for a torpedo workshop. We flew back to Sydney and started organizing. Colonel Ray Elsmore, Ass't. Chief of Staff, turned out to be our best ally. He opened many doors as did Commander Kelly. The RAAF was a pain in the neck continually gumming up the works as fast as Fuz and I straightened them out.

We had conference after conference with RAAF big shots.

General Brett's word was, "Get along with the RAAF with patience as best you can." The young men of the RAAF are magnificent. Their active pilots are as fine as any in the world and have performed deeds of heroism that would curl the hair of the most calloused if ever told. At Perth there was a pilot who was the surviving member of a squadron that combated Zeros, at Rabaul in a plane like our AT-6, North American trainer – another, Tom Watson, a Canadian who has been shot down in Spitfires over the Channel, in Brewster Buffaloes over Singapore, in P-40s over Java, and is still raring to go. In spite of the "old school" types at the top, the RAAF runs damn well because of these fighting chaps. Australia is like that. Finally the orders were written for some pilots from the group to report to Nowra with their airplanes for torpedo training.

Nowra is about 125 miles south of Sydney near Jervis Bay. It went operational in May 1942. As the shore base facility for Carrier Air Groups. Number 6 Operational Training Unit was formed here. Aircraft units training here were using Bristol Beauforts and B-26 Marauders. Six planes and seven crews from the 22nd BG arrived for training during July and August 1942. The 19th BS unofficially was called the "1st Torpedo Squadron." An instructor recalls, "The attack techniques were as spectacular as they were dangerous. We flew so low that the slipstream threw up great rooster tails of water behind us. We trained to drop in point-blank range of enemy guns."

The local Nowra newspaper wrote: "Yesterday morning when the 'birds' came home to roost, they skimmed the tops of houses in town, much to the alarm of residents. Among the complaints received was: choice lemons were blown off trees in the garden." Pilots had mixed feeling about torpedo launching and thought the whole idea was a 'lemon.' Erroneous reports of success at Midway were misleading and the need for crews to rejoin their squadrons up north was urgent. Captain Allen had done a highly commendable and sometimes frustrating job. Other Groups and the RAAF continued torpedo training but by 1944 it was apparent torpedo operations were dropping away." No.6 OTU was disbanded 31 March 1944.

Editor's note: Here ends Captain Allen's tale of: trials, tribulations, testing and teaching torpedo techniques to a gaggle of land-based airplane drivers. He turns the chore over to others and plots a course to Adelaide to pick up Lt. Cooper and head north – back to the war – meanwhile "I got a wire from Cooper. He'd done it again!" It seems he'd taken off from Adelaide and was halfway to Melbourne when an engine failed. He flew back over the mountains on one engine and made a good landing at Adelaide. Unfortunately the field was wet, and he slid into a bad spot and the nose gear collapsed – the price, two new engines and props – at least it wasn't his fault this time. He'd done a nice job of it. On 23 August 1942 Allen and Cooper rejoin the 19th Bomb Squadron at **Woodstock** and remained operational there until 15 September 1942 when the squadron moved operations north to **Iron Range:** Only a short 60 minute flight across the Coral Sea to Port Moresby, New Guinea. We take leave of Captain Allen – temporarily – we'll rejoin him as he and his B-26 – **Sea Wolf** – prepares to bomb enemy-held East Timor by way of Batchelor Field, Darwin, 1,200 miles west of Marauder home-fields near Townsville on the Coral Sea coast. Meanwhile, 1st Lt. Merrill Dewan continues our story in **Chapter 12.**

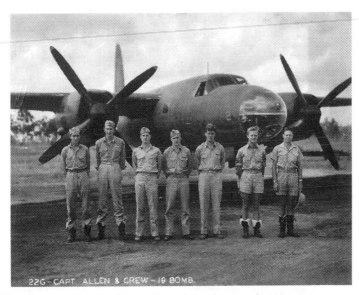

"Sea Wolf" crew: Left to Rt. Sgt. Charles Jordan, turret gunner; Sgt. Woodrow Brakefield, engineer; Lt. Charles Smith, navigator; Capt. Frank Allen, pilot; Capt. Charles Eberly, bombardier; Sgt. Americus Holden, radio operator; Sgt. Lawton Harrum, crew chief.

Marauder engine run-up on an edge-of-jungle "hard-stand" at *Iron Range* airdrome, York Peninsula, Queensland, Australia – just a 60 minute flight over the Coral Sea to Port Moresby, Papua New Guinea.

"Sea Wolf" gunner, Sgt. Charles Jordan "bagged" a Japanese "Zero" and is rewarded with a plane silhouette painted under his gun turret. Proud, Marauder pilot, Captain Frank Allen points to the award.

"Old 1491" sister-ship of "Calamity Charlie", stuck in the mud – nose gear collapsed, props were bent backward. She'll be out of service for a-while getting new engines and other repairs so guns are removed for safe-keeping.

"Sea Wolf", Capt. Allen's plane sadly sits in the salvage yard. After surviving 19 bombing missions and flights to exotic destinations, she met her fate while on loan piloted by a new crew. As time goes by Allen will name other ships "Sea Wolf II through IV. They were flown here in the Southwest Pacific and in the ETO thus, racking up a total of 57 combat missions.

"Camera! Action!" Squadron Commander, Lt. Col. Frank S. Allen, Jr. Pilot and part-time photo-journalist is proud of his pilot wings and his sharpshooter badge. Pointing his Leica he shouts, "Just one more!" – and shoots. The result – several shots in this book were taken by "Chief" Frank Allen.

"Pistol-packin'-sharp-shooter" Lt. Col. Frank Allen, is on the practice range sporting the cannonball pocket-patch emblem of his 598th Bomb Squadron, 397th BG, 9th Air Force in Europe.

Editor's note: Let's meet 1ˢᵗ Lt. Merrill T Dewan, a keen observer and prolific writer as seen in his "Red Raider Diary" published by his son Tom Dewan.

Chapter Twelve

Battle Stations – Reid River – Iron Range

This is 1ˢᵗ Lt. Merrill T. Dewan's Story

Lt. Merrill T. Dewan is a B-26 Navigator in the 22ⁿᵈ BG – 18ᵗʰ BS, flying from a backwater airfield in Australia called **Reid River,** where he and his squadron mates are literally "camping." We are privileged to share select entries from his "Red Raider Diary" – words that describe endless oceans, sweating jungle, enemy air raids, deadly combat and happy rides on the 'Toonerville-trolley' to Townsville, a small port city on the Coral Sea, we share his delight in meeting 'Aussies.' By his words we feel the strain of battle, share his poignant observations, his courageous, sometimes sentimental passion for people around him. His narrative is reminiscent of James Michener's Nobel Prize novel *Tales of the South Pacific.* But Merrill's narrative is not fiction; it's about real people – about what really happened to them. We cheer the "can-do-make-do" spirit that prevailed during those desperate early days of World War Two in the South Pacific.

Lt. Dewan's 18ᵗʰ BS and Lt. Frank Allen's 19ᵗʰ BS are part of the 22ⁿᵈ Bombardment Group (22ⁿᵈ BG) at Langley Field, Virginia. Being in different squadrons, they may not have met however, after December 7ᵗʰ, – Pearl Harbor – their mobilization experiences are the same; they sail together to Hawaii on the USS Grant. The 19ᵗʰ BS was the lead squadron, first to go island hopping across the Pacific to Australia. Lt. Allen took off 17 March 1942 and reached Brisbane 20 March 1942. Lt. Dewan's 18th BS stayed in Hawaii doing additional operational training flying B-18s while their B-26s are reassembled. They started island hopping nearly a month later on 12 April 1942 and reached Brisbane 1 May 1942. In his Red Raider Diary on May 8, Merrill briefly describes his island hopping experience. "We spent three weeks trying to get to Australia…had engine trouble all the way. At Canton Island we spent two weeks under horrible conditions…Canton Island sits on the equator and the temperatures get to 127 (degrees)…spent three days each on New Caledonia and in Fiji…saw an awful lot of water – this Pacific is huge!"

Editor's note: Battle Stations – Reid River and Iron Range – We follow B-26 action by linking Merrill's and Frank's diary notes and letters. The 22nd BG flew their first combat mission – Sunday, 5 April, 1942 – target was Rabaul, New Britain. Merrill's 18th BS flew their first mission five weeks later on Monday 11 May 1942. Both were flown from Townsville, Garbutt Field while other Battle Stations were being built. See: Appendix G. Captain Frank Allen, finished his special Torpedo testing assignment and returns to action with the 19th BS on 23 August 1942. Thanks to Merrill's diary and Frank's letters we are, in a literary sense, "where the action is."

Merrill describes – *Iron Range* – in the jungle of Cape York Peninsula, a one-hour flight across the Coral Sea to Port Moresby, "What a helluva hole! Our camp at *Reid River* is paradise compared to it. It is in thick tropical jungle. The nearest town is 130 miles away – Cooktown population 150 – there is no road to it. We flew right over it and couldn't see it. The campsite is so deep-in it is like dusk all the time." Merrill describes his camp, *Reid River,* home of the 18th BS 35 miles south of Townsville, "It's a little old field way back in the woods right on the bank of a pretty large stream and we've got a reg'lar old swimmin' hole. We can swim, bathe, and wash our clothes and fish. The boys built themselves an Officers'

Club made of logs with a bar – we take turns bar tending – we have electricity and a radio – it's a place to relax after bombing missions."

For a time-frame reference, visualize: the **Battle of the Coral Sea** raging, May 4 – May 7, 1942 (***Appendix F***) and the 22BG is fully engaged. It is a busy time: May 8, Merrell is promoted to 1 st Lt. – On May 10, Allen is promoted to Captain. News of the Coral Sea battle is reported in Australian newspapers; the *Perth Daily News* tells about B-26 aircraft shooting down seven Zeros in five minutes. Allen writes: "I always thought our ships and gunners were good but this exceeds my expectations." He continues, "I'm anxious to get back into the swing again with the rest of the outfit but we'll have to complete this testing mission first." His torpedo drop testing is progressing well. Meanwhile 1st Lt. Dewan writes:

Friday May 8, 1942 I was sworn in as First Lt. I wired Mother Howe and Mother Dewan, Mother's Day cable grams: Took a swim down in our 'swimmin' hole.' Saturday, May 9, Some of the Group went on a mission…terrific battle going on not far from here. It involves the Japanese, American and Australian Navies and Air Forces. The Group sank two ships. May 10, went to Port Moresby (700 miles from Townsville) on the island of New Guinea, and stayed overnight, preparatory to a raid which we do tomorrow. We slept on a wing of the airplane because the mosquitoes were so bad near the ground we couldn't sleep anywhere else… primitive conditions…Very poor food.

A sleek-stripped-down "Straight" B-26 Marauder doing a dusty run-up at *Reid River.*

Laloki landing strip, Port Moresby, Papua New Guinea – a carpet of Pierced Metal Matting.

Editor's note: *These are called "leap-frog" missions. Because of great distances and the need to carry an effective bomb load, refueling is done at an intermediate airfield close to the battle zone. Facilities are primitive at Port Moresby and it is constantly under attack.*

Monday May 11, 1942 we took off at 6:00 A.M. without any breakfast and flew to the city of Rabaul on New Britain Island (500 miles from Port Moresby) and bombed a Jap airdrome there. We blew up a hangar and several airplanes on the ground. I was terribly scared over the target; in fact I was paralyzed with fear – as were we all. None of the famous Jap Zero fighters attacked us. Anti-aircraft fire missed us, thank God. We came back to Port Moresby and landed to gas up, but Barney wasn't with us. He couldn't get his bomb doors closed after he dropped his bombs and we had to leave him. As we were "gassing-up" we saw Barney come wobbling in to land, and just then an air raid took place and we all scattered to the hills running for our lives. Poor Barney was attacked as he was landing and his tail gunner was killed. Barney got a bullet in his arm, and his navigator got shrapnel in his arms. All are in the hospital. Our pursuits shot down the three "Zero" fighters who attacked Barney. It was a furious aerial battle, with the "Zeros" attempting to strafe our ships on the ground and P-39s fighting to protect us. They chased them away – we took off and came home to – Australia and Reid River. Oh God, how good and peaceful it looked for to-nite. I was unnerved as well as physically worn out.

This evening the Enlisted men hosted a spaghetti supper. It was excellent – made me homesick. One of my periodic duties is censoring enlisted-men's outgoing mail, reading the private lives of the men. Actually you just skim over the page looking for words that might betray location or operational activity. Officers' outgoing mail also gets skimmed.

Editor's note: *Merrill's diary describing everyday events gives us a feeling of 'you-are-there' a taste of life the way it was – young men far from home adjusting to warfare – endless ocean, sweating jungle, repetitive waiting, strange cultures, performing low key heroics. We are absorbed in his candid observations, clear and lasting.*

We went out to the strip where a 2ⁿᵈ Squadron's B-26 was trying to land with his landing gear retracted – since he couldn't get it down and land safely. After circling for two hours he finally got it down and landed safely – some sweet job. Some sort of damn animal – like a small bear – got inside my tent and woke me up scuffing around. I chased him outside and around the tent three or four times, with a flashlight in one hand and my 45 automatic in the other – and with not a stitch of clothing on!

Tuesday June 9, 1942 – We've been put on special "alert" and cannot leave the camp area. A damn kangaroo got inside my tent last night, when I chased him I fell over a box in the doorway and almost broke my neck – between the Aussie bear and the kangaroo – I'm going crazy! A whole gang of Coast Artillery just moved in to guard our runway.

Saturday May 16, 1942 – Four of our planes left for Townsville to go on a mission today. My ship went but Doc wouldn't let me go, gave me some medicine and sent me to my tent. Our boys were to "gas-up" (It's only 35 miles away), load some bombs and fly across the Coral Sea to Port Moresby, remain there over-night, then take off at dawn and bomb either Lae Airdrome on the north side Jap-held coast of New Guinea or the airdrome at Rabaul, New Britain occupied by the enemy. Something happened; they didn't go and returned to Reid River. Yesterday however, three B-26s from 19th BS bombed Rabaul, and were attacked by five Zero fighters and two German Messerschmitts. The three B-26s shot all seven of them down and did their bombing. OH! Our plane is very safe! Once it gets into the air because it is awfully fast and is bristling with guns. But, it's terribly dangerous if power is lost during takeoff mode; it's killed over 75 men in our 22 BG already. But the amazing thing is that only one B-26 has actually been shot down by the enemy.

Tuesday May 19, 1942 – Our airplanes are grounded – gas tank problem. So we had the day off. Foggy and I are quite the "slickers" in horseshoe pitching. We beat all comers. It's one of our pastimes when we are on alert. Sometimes we swim in the creek – but now that's barred because they found the water to be heavily contaminated – so we pitch horseshoes.

Saturday May 23, 1942 – Got up early – loaded bombs at Townsville. There were three of us, Massie, Michaelis and us. Burrough (navigator) was with Michaelis… took off for the "hot spot' – Port Moresby – incidentally our 22nd Bomb Group (what's left of it) is keeping PM from being taken. We got up there about four o'clock, got our ships gassed-up and went up to camp for supper. What a hole this place is! The poor devils that are stationed here! They are all jittery and half shell-shocked from being bombed. The food is awful and the mosquitoes are terrible, but we managed to get some sleep in an overcrowded, stuffy old tent. We got up at 0400 and had a sorry breakfast, three of the 33rd BS were supposed to go with us on the mission but they didn't get off, we three went on alone. Our objective was Rabaul. We hit the airdrome at 1030 on Sunday morning, the church hour at home.

We ran into a terrible barrage of anti-aircraft fire blossoming around us. Michaelis got hit in three places. Massie got hit in his right engine and we had to drop back and decrease our speed so he could stay with us. But his engine finally cut out entirely and then he tried to fly on one engine. But he kept going lower & lower, losing altitude, and finally called us on the radio, and told us he couldn't stay in the air any longer – and said he was going to crash it on the beach in New Britain. This was the last we heard from him, the last anyone has heard. Perhaps he crashed in the water. I pray not. If they did land on New Britain, they are all prisoners now. Michaelis managed to limp back to Port Moresby with us and his engine cut out when he landed. Burrough was hit by a piece of shrapnel in his arm. Our plane wasn't hit at all, which is a miracle. We led the way home, then when we got near Port Moresby we were scared there might be an air raid, but fortunately there wasn't. So we landed. Mike's ship was a shot-up mess and he was extremely lucky to have made it this far. So he stayed. We – one remaining ship – only us – refueled and took off for Townsville. We made it by 5:00 PM – a nervous, sad bunch of boys – for although we had done great damage at Rabaul, started fires, blown up hangars and airplanes, we also had been shot-up and lost eight of our comrades.

Editor's note: Survivors Sighted – *To follow-up on the fate of the crashed crew described above we **jump ahead** 10 months to read… March 21, 1943…Merrill's words:*

A remarkable thing has happened! A small number – 4 or 5 – white men have been sighted on the north coast of New Britain, near where Hal Massie & crew went down when they were with us nearly a year ago. One of our reconnaissance planes saw them, they flashed a serial number on a big cardboard, and it turned out to be Lt. Wallace's – Massie's co-pilot! Now 5th Bomber Command will try to affect a rescue. Colonel Devine (Former 22 BG CO.) is in charge. The plan: A massive raid on Rabaul to divert attention while a boat picks up the men. It is our prayer that it works! It will be a sensation! I hope it isn't a trap. (*Next entry*) Thursday March 25, 1943, a miraculous thing happened last night! They rescued part of Hal Massie's crew! He must have crash-landed on the beach, almost 10 months ago to the day, three were killed but Lts. Massie, Wallace, King, Hughes and Sergeant Bordner survived. Later on, Massie and King were captured by a Jap patrol. The other three evaded capture and lived 10 months in the jungle with a native tribe! They were spotted, last week, on the beach only 100 miles from the powerful Jap base at Rabaul.

They were waving frantically to the American plane. He dropped a note telling them to be there next day, same time. Next day, the Recon-Bomber dropped them a paint brush, a can of black paint and four white bed sheets with instructions to paint the serial number of the ranking man on a sheet. Next day the plane returned and photographed them – the number proved to be Lt. Wallace's. The Recon ship went back yesterday and the message told them to be ready to be rescued last night. At night, an Aussie flying boat sneaked in, landed and picked them up while a terrific attack was in progress on Rabaul. This morning they are here safe in Port Moresby. Unbelievable! Wonderful!! They are surrounded by a bunch of generals so I couldn't get to talk with them. They will be sent back to the States, but I hope they get down to the Squadron to see their buddies before they go.

(**Next entry**) Sunday March 28, 1943 – at noon-time our rescued buddies arrived from Port Moresby. What a reception we gave them! After 10 months with native tribesmen in the jungles of New Britain, they were tickled to be back with their old Squadron mates. Of course they won't stay long. We had lots of pictures taken with them and we spent all afternoon and evening listening to their stories. Lts. Massie and King were betrayed by some natives and turned over to the Japs. Sgt. Swan survived but died of malaria on October 20. Newsreel cameramen and reporters had been dogging them in PM (Port Moresby), but not here. God has blessed them. Monday March 29 – News from Port Moresby – General Ramey, CO of the 5ᵗʰ Bomber Command, is missing. He was in a B-17 doing recon. work, in New Guinea, and the plane failed to return. That makes the third General we've lost in this theater. Not a very good record. Everyone liked General Ramey; these generals, should lay-off this damn combat flying.

Editor's note: Returning to May entries. After the ill-fated mission to Rabaul in which Massie crash-landed on a New Britain beach – Merrill is minus one tent mate, Lt. M. C. Hughes, who was navigating for Massie.

Friday May 29, 1942 – Foggy & three of our ships were supposed to execute a series of night raids against Lae. He came back because his ship hadn't gotten off the ground, so he and I went to town, Townsville, on the train after dinner. We stayed at the Great Northern Hotel. He had a date and I went to the movies – An American film – *I Wanted Wings*… ironic. We returned on the 6:30 pm train took only two hours to get here. That's record time for the Reid River – "Stragglin' Steamliner" – 35 miles in 2 hours.

Tuesday June 2, 1942 – Something big is cooking – I think – rumor is that they are assembling all the airplanes they can up in this territory; there may be a push in the making. We are keeping Port Moresby from being taken and they are building it up stronger every day, more supplies moving in, more anti-aircraft being established. It's our only remaining airbase in New Guinea. By holding it we could start a "push" northward, retake Rabaul (on the island of New Britain). Burrough and I went to Townsville and got paid. I drew 1ˢᵗ Lt. pay since May 5, $233, cabled Elsie $160, paid off depts. – meals – lodging – laundry – loaned out some money and still have thirty dollars left. I could get by on $5 or $10 a month easily – outside of meals.

Saturday June 6, 1942 – Foggy and I each took one of the new Aussie Sergeant-Navigators up for a familiarization ride in the B-26 – flew around the vicinity of Reid River and Townsville, and gave them practice using our equipment. They seem to be pretty keen, eager to learn. My friend – Robert – was spell-bound at what he termed "marvelous and elaborate equipment" of the B-26. He was amazed at the great speed and his eyes were as big as saucers when he saw the Airspeed Indicator registering 230 & 240 mile per hour in level flight. We landed at 10:30 because I had to get my laundry in Townsville…going to catch the 11:00 train in Reid River. It was late…by two hours…so I walked down the dusty road until I was picked up by an American truck…got my laundry…came back on the 5:00 PM truck that always comes every day from there to the 18ᵗʰ camp (408ᵗʰ – pardon me!! They changed our designation from 18ᵗʰ.)

Sunday June 14, 1942 – Borrowed a truck from Transportation and went down the creek bed a mile or so and got a load of sand for my tent floor…makes an excellent floor…keeps down the dust and keeps the bugs off the bed. On mission tomorrow…a rather ticklish one – going to bomb Lae…means more scraps with those damnable

"Zeros"! I'm going to try a hand at gunnery. Going to operate the .50 caliber turret gun – I'd like to shoot down a "Zero" or two. We'll sneak in over the Owen Stanley Mountains which separate the north and south shores of New Guinea.

Wednesday June 17, 1942 – I'm back safely. We left Reid River Monday morning and four of us (ships from the old 18th) flew to nearby Garbutt Field in Townsville. Here we joined eight other 22BG ships and loaded bombs, each ship carrying 30 – one hundred pound bombs, ate dinner and took off for Port Moresby. It took us 3 hours to get there; 650-700 miles straight north across the Coral Sea. We arrived about 4:30 PM. They hadn't had a raid in two weeks. Surprisingly conditions are much improved. We found the natives had built the Air Corps grass huts to sleep in – nice ones – a great improvement of the old musty tents we slept in before. They even had showers! We all got cleaned up. And then another surprise – excellent food! What a change from just five weeks ago (*May 8 entry*) when we had to fly a mission without breakfast. We had a briefing after supper.

Editor's note: Maximum effort – *Merrill is back in Port Moresby. A combined 5th Air Force maximum effort was underway. These are designed to reduce the enemy's ability to air attack the landing of Marines, scheduled for 7 August, on Guadalcanal 700 miles south of Rabaul in the Solomon Islands. The route between scattered islands is "the Slot" where Navy PT boats linger to attack Jap convoys near "Iron Bottom Bay."*

Monday June 15, 1942, evening briefing included crews from B-25s and B-17s that would be working the "show", also the P-39 (Aerocobras). The B-25s were to attack the airdrome at Salamaua, New Guinea while we and the B-17s (Flying Fortresses) were attacking the stronger airdrome at Lae. We rose early Tuesday June 16, 1942, morning to stand by our planes to take off in case of a raid. And it did come. At 0830 the alarm sounded; everybody started running. Most of our crew were scared to death, and forgot all about the airplane, and beat it for the bomb craters and slit trenches up in the woods. All that was left in our crew was pilot, co pilot, bombardier and me. All the planes, B-17s, B-25s, B-26s and P-39s got off except two before the Jap planes arrived. We flew out to sea and flew around in the clouds for two hours until we received the "all clear" over the radio. Then we returned. I had been power-turret gunner; Hall the bombardier was tail gunner. We landed and all 30 mixed planes gassed up ready to go – of course our time had been set back because of the raid.

Fifteen enemy planes had come over – all "Zeros" – no bombers. They were very high – our pursuits kept them up there. They had seen no planes on the ground so they probably went back and told their HQ at Lae that they need not fear a raid. But, alas they were caught with their pants *(planes)* down. After we had landed and gassed up we left the ground at intervals – 12:00 to 12:35 PM – It took us 1½ hours to reach our target, Lae. We circled around and approached Lae from the north. Three flights of four ships came in from slightly different directions, crisscrossing the airdrome, each flight dropping its 120 bombs on a predetermined target. Our 18th BS flight went right down the hangar line – just like they did on the hangar line at Hickam on December 7th. It made my heart feel good to see these buildings blow up. I always go back in the Bomb Bay and write "Regards from . . . " Or other words, on the first "egg" to be dropped.

Our ship got a bullet hole. As we passed over the target I went into the back of the ship and got on one of the guns *(waist-gun position at an open window)*. By the time we reached the target there were "Zeros" everywhere – but we were flying such a close formation they didn't dare come in close because of our concentrated fire power. One "Zero" came up towards me on our right side and I let him have it with a burst from the .50 caliber machine gun – those red tracer bullets making pretty, but deadly red streaks towards him – and he rolled over in the air and "beat it." Those "Zero" fighters are excellent – very fast and much more maneuverable than our pursuit – and they are all colors. Some are painted red, others blue – others grey, etc. It was while I was bent over shooting at this Jap fighter I nearly fell out of the airplane (and I didn't have a "chute" on!) As it was I had a picture of Elsie in the upper pocket of my flying suit – and the suction from the open gun window drew it right out! So, Elsie, you are now at the bottom of the sea somewhere north of New Guinea.

We fought our way back towards the place where our P-39s were lurking in ambush – on the way one smart guy in a "Zero" thought he would sneak up and get us from behind – he got a blast from all four tail gunners – and he too is now at the bottom of the sea. There were 15 to 20 "Zeros" alongside us on both sides – but two or three miles off – but they would not come in to attack – so we led 'em smack into those lurking P-39s. As we passed the soupy cloud area we called out on the radio – "Rainbow from peanuts – we are here, and we've got company." Before the "Zeros" caught on, the P-39s were diving on them and they shot down three before the others knew what was happening. Good old pursuit cover. It's the first time we've had it. Even the Japs won't bomb Port Moresby without protective escorts. Before this mission good 'ole 22BG did it time and time again – all alone. We got safely back to our over-nite home – Port Moresby – all ships in the Group – ate supper and went to bed exhausted. We got up at dawn (Wednesday) just in case the Japs tried an attack while we were on the ground. It didn't happen.

Wednesday June 17, 1942, it took us three hours to reach Townsville. We flew directly over the town and then on to our camp at Reid River and each of us gave the camp area a "buzz" at 300 miles an hour right over the tree tops! If we were a Fighter Group we'd have done a victory roll. When we got on the ground and back to the camp area they were having a "barbeque and beer bust" – everyone was "high" including O'Neill, the CO. Everyone shook our hands and slapped us on the back – tickled to see us back safely. I cannot describe the anxiety the boys on the ground sincerely feel for us when we are gone. They show it in their faces when we return. It's just like a big family – we were so tired and filthy with long beards so we soon retired and went to bed.

Thursday June 18, 1942, Foggy and I got up early and took the train to Townsville…3 long hours this time…had a good steak dinner…still can't get milk…haven't had a glass of milk since leaving Hawaii. In the evening we were invited to the home of Foggy's girl friend. I chatted with the "old folks" while Foggy and Miss. Gallager, "discussed the weather" in the parlor. Barney, the Dad, enjoyed American cigarettes and I heard all about sheep shearing on cattle stations in the 'Out Back'. We left about 11:30…stayed at the Great Northern Hotel. We are here on a long week-end. Friday afternoon we went to a movie, *Under Two Flags*, the newsreel featured combat crews and John O'Connell's B-26 was in it and the name, "Goosey Lucy" stood out clearly. John never put the "Goosey" in front of his girl's name some, joker did it and he was afraid his girl would see it and be sore. Our stay was a change from tent-city, squadron chores and the next mission.

Thursday June 25, 1942 – Just before leaving for Port Moresby on a bombing mission we have been told that our 22 BG have been the most effective outfit so far. We've averaged downing eight pursuit "Zeros" to one B-26 shot down. Congratulations came from General Britt – thanks to our fire-power and "dead-eye" gunners.

Saturday June 27, 1942 – At Port Moresby: Last night the weather was so bad we couldn't get over the mountains to bomb Lae. ***Editor's note:*** *The Owen Stanley Mountains form a back-bone ridge on New Guinea. Japs hold Lae on the north shore, we hold the south shore; the location of Port Moresby. There is one "impossible" trail through the mountains linking Lae to Port Moresby area. Fierce fighting occurred in the mountain pass. Aussies successfully prevented a break-through.* We sat around all day today waiting to mount a night raid. At 1:00 PM we were raided and barely got our planes off the ground in time – flew them out over the ocean until we got the "All Clear" and we came back and landed.

After supper I was milling around by the plane, in the dark, when all of a sudden a great flare came shooting down out of the sky and lit up the whole airdrome. I knew it meant Jap bombers and bombs would fall immediately on the flare. They did – didn't have time to be scared. I made a running dive right into a "foxhole" I remembered just 50 feet from the plane. I didn't dare raise my head. Then "Whoosh!" It sounded like a 4th of July skyrocket uncomfortably close – then the most staggering, deafening and earth-shocking explosion that I have ever known. The first baby must have been a 2,000 pounder. Its concussion broke window lights in buildings ¼ mile away. It raised me right up off the dirt floor of the trench and dazed me for an instant; Thank God I was in the trench and not on top of the ground. I could see, out the corner of my eye, red-hot pieces of shrapnel sailing across the top of the trench, waist high. It would have blown me to bits if I had been standing up. I was still dazed from the first bomb, and then came a second and another until a dozen had been dropped. Luckily they dropped farther away each time. I heard the planes… big flying boats just right for carrying huge bombs. Our anti-aircraft guns opened up on them; searchlights converged on the three planes. I heard later one was hit and plunged into the ocean nearby.

I climbed out of the trench and found our ship: "Blue Grass Bettye" had been blown around 90 degrees to her former position and there was a big hole caused by shrapnel in her side. We had the hole patched and got off. This time we got through the mtn. pass, but the weather over Lae was terrible – couldn't see a thing – we were over the target, the airdrome, before we knew it. The anti-aircraft opened up on us. This marked the field for us, lights from their guns, so we let them have it – 3,000 pounds of bombs – then all hell broke loose, our left engine started popping and we commenced going around in a wild uncontrollable circle towards the ground. I was being thrown from one side of the plane to the other before I realized we had been hit. May and McCutcheon were fighting hard at the controls to bring "Blue Grass Bettye" out of what was surely a deadly tail-spin if it weren't checked. All the time we were losing altitude right next to the Jap airdrome. We were scared to death. I helped them fight the controls like demons for long sweating seconds. Finally at 1,000 feet we managed to pull her out and began to level off. It had been horrible, like a nightmare in the black of night and we still had a bad left engine.

Our problem now, was to get home; one engine to take us 300 miles. We gained altitude slowly, carefully – to 10,000 feet – we got back across the mountains safely – but we'd aged 10 years in doing it. We landed safely at Port Moresby with a shot-up engine and an unnerved crew of boys. We were shaking like leaves when we got out of the plane. But thank God we were safe. What a night… we slept very little in spite of weariness. Thank God my navigating was on the money over those high mountains. Next morning they were working on our plane. By afternoon it was suitable to fly back to the mainland (Australia). We arrived in Townsville – Reid River – after a three hour hop across the Coral Sea. We were dead tired – got the usual welcome by the boys… glad to see us back safely – it had been a narrow escape… too narrow. Slept after supper until next mid-morning.

Monday July 6, 1942, **Muri Midway** – Rained all day – I mean rain! These tropical rains are terrific. Stayed inside my tent all the time except to go down to the mess tent to eat…heard that Jim Muri had been in the Midway battle (a month ago); he dropped a torpedo out of his B-26. Good old Jim! I'd give a lot to see him! *Editor's note: Jim Muri and Merrill Dewan married their sweethearts, Alice (Susie Q) Moyer and Elsie Howe, in a duel ceremony on Christmas Day, December 25, 1941 in Tucson, Arizona during final stateside training prior to going overseas.*

Tuesday July 7, 1942, Rain subsided at about noon and the boys returned from their 4ᵗʰ of July mission up north. Merrill was not on this mission but describes what happened. "All four ships returned safely – thank God. They all look haggard and weary, but were, as usual, happy. They had really dealt out damage to the Japs, at Lae and at Salamaua. But they caught hell while on the ground at Port Moresby. The Japs retaliated and bombed them continuously – both day and night – two Aussies were killed because they didn't get to the slit trench soon enough. O'Neil's airplane was burned up on the airdrome by an incendiary bomb. During our raid on Lae just after they dropped their bombs and turned away, a "Zero," trying to intercept them, was killed by our gunners, his plane, out of control crashed freakishly, ill-fatedly, crashed into Mo Johnson's airplane – in midair – both went down in flame into the ocean – more bad luck for our Bomb Group – Its rapidly being cut to pieces. I was bar tender for the gang after supper and they really drank, there were lots of stories about close calls during their mission.

Sunday July 12, 1942, Felt lousy all day… in the afternoon our combat crew had its picture taken… went over to the newly built darkroom to learn how to make pictures. We can develop pictures of airplanes, of combat, or anything we want too that censors previously wouldn't let anyone develop for us. But we must keep them in our own possession. In the afternoon we were notified we were to go to Sydney, or near there for gunnery school.

Editor's note: *From July 14, for six weeks until September 2, Merrill is attending a gunnery school. He didn't say how many are attending from the 22 BG. Classes don't start until August 1, so the school CO gave them leave. I will combine some of Merrill's diary entries to give a rounded account of his sojourn. He wrote:*

On TDY (Temporary Duty) Start: Wed., July 15, 1942, "Blue Grass Bettye" was in the mood to go so we hopped off to Brisbane and remained over-night (RON) – all our crew stayed at the same hotel – I almost froze – it's winter down here… flew south to, Williamport; (Gunnery School) 70 miles north of Sydney & New

Castle... took the school CO (he's English) down to Melbourne. This is really down south – as far south of the equator as New York is north of the equator. It's mid-winter and awfully cold...July 21, flew back to Williamtown, another Colonel, an advisor at the school, came with us...met an old friend, Biddenger, from Lyons Falls, NY, a Sgt. at the school. I spent the rest of my leave in New Castle, a cute little hotel overlooking the Pacific Ocean, cheaper than in Sydney, airplane Ferry pilots from states stay here so l hear "what's new at home." ... feeling mentally rested except – heard of new threat on Port Moresby – 22 BG is carrying 50% of the attacks on invading Jap fleet in New Guinea.

School classes start today, Sat., Aug. 1, 1942; 8 hrs/per day, as far as I can see they're not valuable to us. It is RAF methods and their guns which we don't use. Barracks beds worse than our bunks up north, hard, thin and cold. Aug. 5, flew, afternoon in a B-17, practice "shooting" at an attacking Brewster Buffalo, a make-believe "Zero" we "shot" with camera... after supper went to movie in New Castle; saw newsreel, Col. Devine belly landing at Port Moresby, his hydraulics had been shot out. We landed just behind him. It was exciting seeing it... more morning classes, then afternoon flying, this time in a British twin-engine Bristol Beaufort – a first for me. Aug. 7, news report U.S. Marines attacking Guadalcanal and our boys up north hitting hard the usual targets... more classes... battle in Solomon Islands raging... stayed overnight at beach hotel. Rushed in taxi to catch ferry just pulling out, made a running leap, missed, and settled like a stone in the icy bay, all passengers watching, embarrassed, crawled out soaked, caught next ferry, missed classes. More late days and the RAF CO is pretty p-o-ed he called us in and bawled the devil out of us... invited to supper at an instructor's home, fun, fine Australian people. I did gun stripping and had oral exams... got our exams marks; I was high American and just slightly under top man an Australian. Went to Sydney, arranged air transportation

back to Townsville… one stop at Brisbane got home at 6:00pm.
Editor's note: *Here ends the Gunnery School sojourn.*

Thursday September 3, 1942, came out to camp in a staff car.
After a month away it was good to get back and see all the boys again.
Johnny Miller was here – he arrived from Hawaii and brought news
that Jim Muri is back in the states that R.O. Miller and others are at
Wheeler Field with their B-26s, sad news that Herb Mayes was killed
in the Midway battle with the rest of his crew. This news shocked
me to my heels. Herb was one of my best friends. Poor Mabel. They
were so marvelous to Elsie – and Herb's folks were, too.

Friday September 11, 1942 – Went into Townsville on the train (The
Stragglin' Streamliner), had supper and talked with a Captain who had
been at Port Moresby. The Japs are only 158 miles away on the other side
of the Owen Stanley Range. Our 19ᵗʰ BS has moved up north farther,
towards them at Cape York Peninsula – north of Cooktown. We are
preparing for an invasion. The 19ᵗʰ BS is ready with its torpedoes.

Editor's note: *The 19ᵗʰ BS had been flying out of **Garbett Field**;
former Townsville Airport, and later at **Woodstock** – now they have
moved to their battle station in the jungle – **Iron Range** – one hour
flying time to Port Moresby. Of colorful interest: It was a sight to see
B-26s taxiing down the street of the Garbutt neighborhood when new
runway facilities were made available at the old Townsville Airport.
The Crew Chiefs had the honor of "driving." Garbutt Brothers were
longtime meat packers that developed the airport and subdivision in the
1920s . . . . a bit of trivia.*

Friday September 18, 1942, Foggy and Dill Ellis & Company
arrived back last night from their mission, unshaven, filthy, gaunt
and exhausted. Half way back from Moresby one engine cut-out;
they flew the last 350 miles on one stinkin' engine. A truck brought
them from Townsville. Fog & I went to town this AM on the train.
We got a little "Lit-up."

Wednesday September 30, 1942, we got three new pilots today.
They moved into a tent right across from Foggy and me. They seemed

like nice guys. . . .Sure are green as new apples. They came in with more paraphernalia than our Squadron Tech. Supply has. Pretty uniforms etc. – oh! Boy! Will that change!

Sunday October 11, 1942, **Its a Boy! Tommy!** I was just sitting down to write a letter to Elsie, when the greatest news arrived. John Augustine rushed over from the Orderly Room with the cable from Mother Howe. It was one of the happiest moments in my life, the other being when Elsie and I were married. It was two minutes before all the boys were grouped around, slapping me on the back – calling me a real man! A few of the smarter ones gave credit to my little wife. In the evening the drinks were all on me – I bought a cool $20 worth – Squadron Commanders and Colonel Givins the Group Commander were there. I must admit I got pretty well soused.

Newlyweds, Lts Dewan, left, and Muri, rt. With wives Elsie and Alice (Susie Q) at Riverside, Ca, June 1942.

Lts. Dewan, left, and O'Connell on leave in Sydney, Australia, early 1943.

Lts. Fogarty and Dewan at their "quarters", *Reid River*, Queensland, Australia.

Navigator, Lt. Dewan, 2nd from left – O'Donnell's crew – *Reid River*. Top cockpit hatches are open because of intense tropical heat. Fall 1942.

Tuesday October 20, 1942, today, rumors are floating fast. Auggie told me. . . .O'Neil is going to be made CO of the 38th Bomb Group and McCutcheon will command the 71st Squadron of that Group . . . and Dill Ellis will be our new Squadron CO . . . some rumors! Well, O'Neil deserves it, especially for his superb work at the head of this Squadron. My tooth hurts so bad I went to bed. I think I will go to Townsville tomorrow and get it snatched out.

Wednesday October 21, 1942, I went to Townsville with Michaelis and Col. Devine . . . had the aching tooth yanked. . . stayed at the American Officer's Club over night. . . saw McCutcheon there, and he confirmed yesterday's rumor…I am sure glad for both him and O'Neil. Mac and I have flown together since a year ago in September, just after the Texas-Louisiana maneuvers. It seems odd that he is going. We had the oldest combat crew in the Air Corps. He asked me whether or not I wanted to go with him to be Squadron Navigator of the 71st Squadron – it would mean a Captaincy – but I don't want it – I don't like the B-25s' vulnerability to the "Zeros" Furthermore, it is not rank that I desire …it is the chance to go home to my little family, and certainly our own 22nd BG will return before the newly arrived 38th BG.

Editor's note: We skip several of Merrill's daily entries where he tells about checking out new crews, doing routine Squadron chores, censoring mail, getting the welcome news – the general gave permission that half the Squadron can go on leave – comments after being in Sydney on leave:

Tuesday November 3, 1942, Finally made it by train from cold Sydney to Brisbane. What a ride! It kept getting hotter as we got farther north. In Brisbane it was hotter than hell. We boys stayed overnight in a Gov't. Billeted Hotel…saw the movie *Eagle Squadron*. Next day our ships were at Amberly Field. Barney and Auggie had flown down to pick us up. We left right after dinner and got back to **Reid River** at 5:30…God, it's hot here!! Sultry, stifling heat!

Sunday November 8, 1942, censored mail nearly all day, this job is really a pain in the ass. Lt. Col. O'Neil visited us… Handcock of the 2nd BS returned from their raid on Darwin – looking O.K. – He was shot down in the water off the Darwin coast last week – he and his crew got out alive. They were in a rubber boat for 16 hours.

Thursday November 12, 1942, Our new crew flew two hours of practice. Our new ship is 1436 the fastest ship in the Group. But actually it is an old crate – just been patched up with parts from other B-26s. But then, **all of our B-26s are old crates** now, anyhow – it is thanks to excellent maintenance by our enlisted ground crew… they keep us flying . . . Foggy moved out today and left a mess in his corner of the tent. *Editor's note: Where he went will be revealed later.*

Friday November 13, 1942, Flew our crew this morning for two hours – fired all guns – practice shooting. 1436 may be an old ship – but it is a fast one – we found out how fast today when a P-40 fighter, trying to stay in formation with us radioed, "I can't cruise as fast as you." He then peeled away. I went back and practiced shooting from waist guns and tail gun positions. I got a lot of red welts on my arms and neck from empty shells dropping on me from the turret as I was firing from the waist gun position.

Tuesday November 17, 1942, Start of **Two Weeks in Port Moresby.** Eight ships from 18th BS. Landed at Lulaki, a new airdrome at PM…very crude…so are the establishments. Outside our tent a torrential tropical rain is pounding, driving hordes of mosquitoes inside. We have a smudge fire built in the middle of the tent – it's almost as unbearable as the mosquitoes… six of us in the tent… Lt's, O'Donnall, Skipper, Calloway, McCord, Limpach and myself – we have to crawl over one another's beds to get to our own. McCord says, "I'm happy because I'm mentioned in Merrill's diary today."… wise twerp!… the boys are lying on their cots jokingly cursing the weather, New Guinea and the war. I'm glad I brought some canned goods from Australia, they'll come in handy. "Port Moresby chicken" (corned beef) we had tonite is going to get very tiresome. We may carry-out a damn attack to-morrow possible against Buna, to help our forces who are closing in on the Nips. P.L. Moore landed safely at 4:30 PM; glad to see him here safely. The weather closed in right after he landed… mosquitoes murdering me.

Wednesday November 18, 1942, Awakened at 0500 by Ray Burrough. Intelligence Officer at Moresby… breakfast…on alert 0900… briefed for a mission… supposed to attack a convoy approaching Lae – transports and destroyers – we went out but with only four ships – Auggie, R.O.Miller, Poppano and O'Donnall (myself). Others did not get off because of engine trouble. We flew number 4 position (Ass-end Charlie) Weather was stinkin'… our radio communication was out – both inter-com and command (between ships) . . . .but we kept going . . . .four B-26s unescorted by fighters. Then our instruments went out … still kept going. We looked for the convoy but didn't find it. Flew the limit of our range… turned back…on the way we knocked out Buna Airdrome – the alternate target – ack-ack wasn't heavy but it was accurate and nearly knocked our tail off. One "Zero" made a pass at us to no effect. We "Sweated out" our gas supply… lousy weather – Owen Stanley Mountains below . . . .not a good place to bail out… forced to go around a batch of bad weather… flying at 14,000 feet… were set to bail out… but finally broke into the clear and landed. After supper we dug a slit trench… "just in case "of an air raid.

Thursday November 23, 1942, The boys bombed Buna in individual ships to-day. Couldn't get through the weather to Lae. O'Donnell couldn't go anyway because he got burned in the face last night – tried to burn the mosquitoes out of the toilet, and the toilet exploded in his face – someone had poured gasoline in it. Everyone was pretty relieved that the weather had kept us from getting to Lae… would have been suicidal… and accomplished little. To-nite I felt lousy – diarrhea all day. Went to doctor over at adjacent camp. He gave me some medicine and told me not to fly for a few days.

Monday November 24, 1942 – Another mission to Buna this AM. I went with O'Donnell, against the doctor's orders. Paid for it, too. Got very sick while we were bombing. Glad to get back to Laloki primitive as it is… slept most of the day… Doc bawled me out… told me to remain on the ground for a time. More medicine… Japs pulled an air raid on us to-nite – about 10:00 o'clock. Bombs dropped on 7-mile airdrome near this one – but I was in the bottom of a slit trench when they came. Only heard them and saw a reflection against the sky as they exploded.

Saturday November 28, 1942, Flew back to **Reid River** to-day. Replaced by 19ᵗʰ Squadron – who arrived just before we left. **Reid River,** raunchy as it is, looked wonderful to us. I led the flight home – 700 miles over the Coral Sea – without a drift meter. Got here O.K. though. Dead tired.

Editor's note: *After a "residency "of two weeks in Port Moresby the squadron enjoys some "lazy days'" restful relaxation even though it is very hot… about 120 degrees in the shade – a trip to Townsville – a movie – a small party at Sea View Hotel Guest House with the boys. A G.I. truck ride with fruit back home – remembering poor Lt. John Lineberger. He is still in the hospital in Port Moresby, with a high fever so Merrill is alone in the tent.*

Thursday December 3, 1942, We enjoyed Thanksgiving in camp to-day – postponed because we were in New Guinea a week ago and could not celebrate – Turkey was good – raisin pie excellent – in the afternoon I worked on the new Officers Club we are building. We all worked. I laid the concrete floor. We personally designed and constructed this club. Even the Squadron Commander worked on it this afternoon. After supper I developed some negatives in our developing tent – pictures taken in Port Moresby – will print them tomorrow.

Friday December 4, 1942 – Man, did it rain last night. Old Reid River has more water in it this morning than it has had in six months. We went up to swing the compass on our old ship, dear old 1436, this morning. Foggy went up to help me, but there were too many clouds out over the ocean so we couldn't do it. With this ocean flying they need to be accurate. We came back and landed. We call old 1436 the Air Corps "mystery ship" (it's a mystery how she flies!) that old clunk has been smashed up twice over here – shot down once, besides. Yet, we still fly it. There is no other B-26 to replace it. The Group used to proudly display its full strength 65 new B-26s, now it has a paltry **29 planes** left – all of which are so old and so battle-scarred that they are fast becoming death traps – 1436 has 10 big patched up holes from "Zero" and anti-aircraft shrapnel. All of us are getting scared of flying these old crates.

"My God! My hat is off to you boys of the 22nd Group." Said a visiting Glenn L. Martin, Tech. Rep. "In America we wouldn't sell these for junk! It is heartbreaking to see such highly trained and experienced crews have to fly combat in these decrepit airplanes." I agree, the boys back in the States should take a look at the odds we have against us. They holler about having to fly brand new B-26s while we "poor boys" fly these wrecks and complain not at all. We are using the first model ever made and we get no spare parts. We have to scrap one plane and use it for spare parts to repair other ships. We do believe he is right. We should either get new planes or be relieved and sent home. The latter would be best for the boys are fast becoming fatigued, both physically and mentally. Lineberger arrived from Port Moresby to-day. He looks pretty white & weak… yet we press on. ***Editor's note:*** *We might add – the planes also look white and weak.*

Monday December 7, 1942, Seems to me – something fairly important – happened a year ago to-day – a year ago to-nite was the most awful night in my life. The turmoil of the country was terrific and we were spending all night preparing to move. Langley Field was in an uproar. Elsie stayed with me for hours that night – sitting outside the hangar in Pete Moore's car just for me, and half freezing. If I thought I loved her then, I should see myself now.

Editor's note: *To-day, being west of the International Date Line in Australia, Merrill's reminiscing is a day early. The calendar is still December 6 back in Pearl Harbor – but don't get technical – this is romantic reminiscing.*

Saturday December 12, 1942, Hotter than hell to-day. We built a dance floor outside the club for the big party to-nite – nurses are being brought out from Townsville and Charters Tower *(another American base)* to celebrate our new club opening. A tipsy time was had by all. Had a good orchestra – about five men to every nurse. We also had good old fashion American hamburgers – onions and all.

Whooping-it-up in the "Wallaby Castle" *Reid River* Officers' Club while bartender, Merrill, "Jo-Jo", Dewan polishes glasses. It was rumored Merrill received his formal bartender training at "Rick's", a saloon in Casablanca.

Playbill announcing **"Bomb-Happy"** – a home-grown, silly-salvo vaudeville show at *Woodstock* Theatre and *Reid River* Amphitheater, April 24 & 25, 1943. – The "house" was over-sold so it's (SRO) Standing Room Only, at both locations.

Tuesday December 14, 1942 – Received a message from Port Moresby – saying our ship 1436 had been shot up during a raid on Lae. Here's the story: The 2nd Squadron borrowed our plane "Calamity Charlie" (1436) – she's been thru more raids than any other ship in the Group… the navigator was seriously injured. That's fate for you – they borrow our plane – use it – and the navigator – at my desk, using my equipment gets hurt – God be with me.

Editor's note: We again peruse several of Merrill's daily diary entries: Old number 1436 is back to be patched up some more, Navigator, Mullancey was seriously, but not critically injured. Merrill is in the hospital with tonsillitis and possibly malaria (not sure)… ward-mates are Infantry officers, Buna battle, half starved, they said: "If it hadn't been for our bombing they wouldn't have advanced an inch." – O'Donnall brought a package – from Alton – a whole bunch of Hershey chocolate bars…what a rarity!… Another plane gone, (1481) R.O.Miller was taking off, about to leave the ground, one tire blew, it veered off into a ditch, all got out unharmed – thank God – just as they made it the plane burst into flames,… after five days in hospital I'm recovered and back at **Reid River.**

Thursday December 24, 1942, Stifling hot as usual. Seems not at all like Christmas. Haven't heard Christmas carols yet. Perhaps Australians don't sing them. Funny how a bunch of boys like us, get homesick to hear Christmas Carols . . . .the boys are drinking . . . .here in the Club to-nite – as usual – a few nurses are here from Woodstock (another near-by base) – Oh, the boys are singing Carols now – must join them – part of 2nd Squadron have come over to enjoy Christmas Eve with us.

Friday December 25, 1942, Cloudy day in camp…somewhat cool – Godsent relief from the usual hot weather. The frequent showers during the day remind me of snow falling in the beautiful Shenandoah Valley or in Boonville. We had a fine dinner. Turkey, cranberry sauce – and trimmings. It was excellent – even if it was "G.I." In the afternoon part of the 19th Squadron landed here on the way back from Brisbane – and we had a little party. After supper I spent the whole evening in my tent writing a very long letter to Elsie – in remembrance of our anniversary… the marriage and unforgettable first night in Tucson, a year ago to-nite.

Sunday December 27, 1942, A new Navigator moved into the tent. Name is Walkup… has been "thru the mill"… was down in the jungle of New Guinea for two weeks – nearly died of thirst and starvation. Natives finally found him, saved him – brought him out to Port Moresby. Weighed 100 pounds when he came in. He had to bail out of a B-25 when they couldn't find Port Moresby. A crocodile attacked him once – but he beat it off. Nice kid. Pretty thin.

Wednesday December 30, 1942, Didn't rain but man, was it sultry . . . .steam from the wet vegetation started rising just like it does in New Guinea. This afternoon we attended a First Aid lecture by Doc Withers in the Club – while we sat listening the perspiration just steamed off us. Doc covered what to do if someone is shot, or if we are forced down in the jungle. We each have a little First Aid Kit in our emergency jungle kits that are tied to our parachutes – bandages, indigo, quinine, scissors, salve and morphine. Very handy. A few Nurses came over to the Club to-nite. The question on everyone's tongue, "What is 5th Bomber Command going to do with us?" – We now have **only 27 *airplanes* in the whole 22nd Group** – all of which are worn out.

Thursday December 31, 1942 – Good bye to the old year! And what a year! The most heartbreaking in my life – the most agonizing – many "close calls" – lots of combat. May God be with me as he did during this year – during 1943 – may he guide me back to my little family safely before too long. And may he do the same for the other boys of our Group. May he see us all home soon, for a well needed and well deserved rest.

Editor's note: *There are many airfields and other American facilities in the vicinity of Townsville. Friends visit each other, some via jeep others fly in. Merrill describes crashes also, "driving down to Woodstock with*

Fred Federle – a bunch of nurses are stationed there. Fred goes with one of them – roads are full of holes two & three feet deep – those poor nurses, what a helluva mud hole they live in – wet, stinking, mosquito-infested. I met sergeant Gysel who used to be my lab. instructor in Botany in college, we had dinner, small world. Most of the boys have gone to Port Moresby – "Doc" says, "No, I can't go." I feel out of place here on the ground. We learn that the boys' stay "up north" is suddenly cut short – there are **now only 16 planes left** *in the 22ⁿᵈ BG.*

Wednesday January 6, 1943, The boys have all gone to Port Moresby – all except Wade Roberts and crew. He has no airplane – I feel lousy sitting here with my gang all up north – feel like I'm a slacker. Damn it! I feel all right – why did "Doc" say 'No' you can't go!"

Saturday January 9, 1943, Captain Crosson's navigator, Grant, from the 2ⁿᵈ Squadron came over and told me about the close shave his crew had last week that should go down in history. Here is his story: They were bombing Lae, when a 3-inch anti-aircraft shell hit them, exploding in the bomb-bay just as they were about to release their bombs. The bomb doors were open – they still had a full load of bombs. The shell nearly blew the plane in two, and it cut nearly all the control cables, smashing the electrical and hydraulic systems. The flaps came down instantly – and the ship started to stall. The wheel was no good so, Capt. Crosson (Jerry) brought it out of the stall with the vertical stabilized control – flew it all the way from Lae to Buna – 200 miles using only rudder and vertical stabilizer – thru heavy rainstorm – made a marvelous crash landing on Buna airdrome – a dirt runway – no one was killed. The ship was smashed to pieces –this airdrome had only recently been taken from the Japs. Grant said he was under two feet of dirt when the plane stopped – plowed in. This speaks well of the strong center keel of the B-26 design.

Monday January 11, 1943, Got a coded message from Port Moresby – our ships were returning and would be here at 12:30 – they arrived right on the dot. All nine of them (not 12) yesterday was a bad day. Our Group lost a whole plane and crew over a Jap convoy. Two more planes made crash landings at Port Moresby – It puzzled us why they were returning so soon. They were supposed to be there at Moresby at least another week or two – found out from them. The whole 22ⁿᵈ Group is now grounded from combat for an indefinite period of time. The whole **Group now has only 16 airplanes left – 16 worn out B-26s.** One of the 19ᵗʰ Squadron's ships with a crew of nine crashed on takeoff at Laloki yesterday. Among those killed were Lt. Hatch & Lt. Sefferin, pilot and co-pilot, the ones written about in the Nov. 14 issue of *"Saturday Evening Post."* I knew them both well. It's another one of those accidents which are going to occur more frequently if we don't quit flying these worn out planes. The usual party to-nite celebrating the boys' safe return was somewhat subdued – rumors flew high and wide.

We now scan Merrill's diary entries of the next few weeks: 3ʳᵈ Group boys from Charter Tower transferred in… said they were tickled to get home… proves what a swell outfit we have… Col. Devine came down from **Iron Ridge**; we flocked around asking about our destiny… he said nothing but we see the 19ᵗʰ BS is moving back to Woodstock only 12 miles away where they were last spring… appears the 22ⁿᵈ Group is being regrouped in one geographic area… started a letter to **Jim Muri** and everyone of the old outfit added to it, even Col. Devine… chores include censoring letters, investigating accidents… Limpach and I are writing awards recommendations including about Col. Devine's 'newsreel' crash landing seen widely in US, Canada and here… only 14 navigators left from my class, counting Foggy and Burrough; rest are dead… Base Censor won't pass crew pictures we wanted to mail home; maybe we look too draggled.

Monday January 25, 1943, Heard the 22ⁿᵈ Group is going to get B-25s. If this is true, then it's the last straw… a rotten deal… the least they can do is give us a decent airplane… we call the B-25 here in this theater…"Zero Bait" or "Flying Paper Bag"… our B-26 is proven, tough, fast, hard hitting, more than a match for wily Jap "Zero" fighters. We have rung up an enviable record of 8 "Zeros" shot down for each B-26 shot down… the Group has done its work saving Australia from invasion this past spring when there was no other Group here to fight. We were in the battles of Rabaul, Lae, Salamaua, Milne Bay, Coral Sea, Buna, and Dilli and the Solomons; now with **only 16 B-26s left** out of 54 we are grounded – tired – weary – and battered. I hope the airplane switch is just a rumor – regardless, we'll keep flying.

Tuesday Jan 26, 1943, Went to Townsville in AM at Intelligence Headquarters and picked up a copy of the Secret Oath for my anti-subversive agents **(*Editor's note*:** *cases of suspected sabotage require counter measures, a bit of internal spying is in-order)* In the afternoon I ran into Elsie's former boss at Langley Field – Captain Milton Hess – we talked nearly all afternoon. He spoke highly of Elsie. I came home after supper.

Editor's note: *For the next six weeks Merrill is doing Squadron administrative work and play. A baseball diamond is built and in the league opener – Navigators beat Pilots 11-10 and enjoyed "riding" them; the pilots were pretty cocky until Foggy hit a homerun. "Slugger" and I celebrated by going to Townsville. Foggy was called to Brisbane. (This, you will recall is when he left the tent in a mess.) Foggy is to navigate none-other than Lt. Gen. George Kenney, big boss of all Air Forces in the Southwest Pacific. My! My! – the Plane – a B-17, with a refrigerator, a gas stove, electric toaster and running water… pretty tough…1ˢᵗ Lt. E.R. Fogarty, you are in for "razzing" when you get back to humble **Reid River**. Had duty (Airdrome Officer of the Day) spent all day chasing pigs, goats, sheep, and cows off the runway in a jeep – maybe if I left them we'd get some decent hamburger. We played the Combat Radio team, won 5 – 1. Went on leave, rode train all night Brisbane to Sydney – arrived at noon, stayed at Combat Officer's Club. Very nice set up, only two shillings a day, meals are only two and three shillings. Spent every day at Bondi Beach, fine powder sand, clear water, almost drowned* *trying to surf board, Sydney harbor is beautiful like a "Travelogue" film in the movies. Long train ride back north, no berths, gee it's hot up here. Boarded the "Stragglin' Streamliner" – 35 miles in 2hrs. – Bunch of new B-25 pilots were riding and they ask all about combat – I felt like an old man – but kind of proud, too.*

Monday March 15, 1943, flew two hours with Dill (Major) Ellis. I flew co-pilot. We had lots of fun buzzing the B-25 training field at Charters Towers, so low we made men scatter in all directions. More mail censoring… one of our planes, number 1427… arrived this evening after its overhauling at the Air Depot… it has all the paint removed and is silver… it is positively beautiful to look at… graceful and so shiny. As more return to the 19ᵗʰ BS it was called "The Great Silver Fleet."

Friday March 19, 1943 – It was cold last night! Tremendous relief… we took off this AM for Port Moresby, Major Anderson, Captain Fletcher, etc. to Bomber Command on official business – but the right engine on dear old 1436 "Calamity Charlie" started spitting hot oil so we had to turn back. We'll go up tomorrow.

Saturday March 20, 1943, Took off at 8:30 AM, had no engine trouble – the Coral Sea was as smooth as glass – landed at 17 Mile Airdrome where O'Neill's 38ᵗʰ Bomb Group is stationed. Ate dinner at 38ᵗʰ HQ Mess… food was excellent, we went to 5ᵗʰ AF Bomber Command HQ and worked with the staff until 8:30 PM… they have a nice set-up in a valley in a big native-built grass hut… cool inside… screened in. Saw a number of friends all captains – ***Editor's note:*** *Merrill writes about promotions in new Groups; if he accepted it would mean staying overseas longer.* He writes: Port Moresby isn't the same Port Moresby of old…back when there was only one Airdrome, dirt at that, and we were bombed daily… food consisted of corned beef & beans. Now, there are at least six Airdromes, powerfully defended… food is excellent… seldom get bombed and each Squadron has an Officers' Club. (***Editor's note:*** *Progress! What a difference 18 months* *makes. It was during this visit Merrill learned of the Rescue we related earlier.)*

Friday April 2, 1943, In camp at **Reid River**. *Editor's note: We will select only the highlights of this eventful month of April.* A list of eligible men to go home was sent to Bomber Command; don't know when that will happen… reported a piece of sabotage to Base Intelligence… One of 38th Group's ships crashed nearby – no survivors… Flew two hours with J.B. Wells who was promoted to first pilot… did a nice job, too… cleared grass around tent since "Fogarty the Firebug" nearly burnt his and Miller's tent down the other day… April 17th flying south to attend Intelligence School – gassed up at Amberly Field, Brisbane, then on to Mascot Field in Sydney, quartered in Metropole Hotel for American Officers while attending school.

Friday April 30, 1943 – After a month flew back to camp, good to be back where it isn't so damn cold. The Group is getting new planes, B-25s. (**The 19th BS will inherit all the remaining B-26s, all 16**)… the Group will move to either Buna on New Guinea or to Goodenough Island NE of Buna. *Editor's note: In 1874 Captain John Moresby, Royal Navy, explored and named the island after his colleague Commodore James Graham Goodenough. The circular shaped island has a precipitous mountain, 8,320 ft. It was known for its gold mines and copra plantations. In August 1943 it became a major troop staging base with hospital, airstrip and 2 Liberty ship wharves: it closed at the end of 1944.* Old personnel of the 22nd Group will be sent home so it will be a younger 22nd Group. We learned why we hadn't been relieved sooner because Washington, DC expected MacArthur and Kenney to turn back the Japanese with a few rickety airplanes and an air force of tired-out boys. Well, we did it. You can't beat Kenney for being a fine general. He's just like one of us. We talked to him just as tho' he were a 1st Lt. instead of a Lt. General. Said about the 22nd Group, "You boys had shot your wad last August when I arrived here, but what could I do? I had no-one to replace you, and was getting no-one and no new airplanes, so I had to hang onto you. When a man has lost the spring in his step it's time he was replaced," he said, "And that is how the 22nd is now." I have the highest respect for this general, because he is "down to earth" honest, sincere and very close to the combat man.

Thursday May 6, 1943, Flew 3 hours 15 minutes this morning in old 40-1549 "Blue Grass Bettye" beat up as she is, she really hopped off the ground – she was showing off for me – 'cause she used to be my plane and it's the first time I've ridden in her for months. In the afternoon, as Intel. Officer, I did an investigation concerning a series of flares that have been shooting around camp. Expect to go into town tomorrow to submit my report. We had free beer party tonight for four crews moving to Port Moresby tomorrow; Col. O'Neil flew down from PM in a B-25 to attend. Half the 2nd Squadron were here – free beer.

Monday May 10, 1943, Spent half the AM cleaning up excess junk. Orders may come through any day now, must take light load for we may fly back in a Liberator, I think. Spent a couple of hours with Lt. Ontank, the new Intelligence Officer, showing him various duties. After dinner taught an Aircraft Identification Class to two crews moving to Port Moresby….gotta get in 45 minutes more flying time tomorrow. **Holy Christ!!! It's happened!!!** Col. Anderson just came in and his executive officer, Major Mansen, read the most wonderful orders ever published!!! Whoopee!! Hot dog!!!! Oh, God, pray thank you from the bottom of my heart. Now, please guide me safely home to my beautiful wife and baby… the orders were read aloud at exactly 0815 PM… **to proceed by air travel to Brisbane, to proceed by air travel to the United States of America…** I'm to leave for Brisbane May 15, (Sat.)

Saturday May 15, 1943, Merrill, Dill, McCord and their enlisted crew plus several from the 2nd Squadron board "Blue Grass Bettye" and land at Amberly Field, Brisbane, had lunch and Merrill wrote: After 14 months Overseas – I reported to 11th Replacement

Center – received orders to leave tonight by B-24 to the States. Depart Australia at 0130 AM Sunday morning and land at 0630 AM at New Caledonia – we're on our way – Island-hopping – **Homeward Bound!**

Chapter Thirteen

Aussie Commandos – Timor Bombing

On 31 October 1942, 22nd BG, B-26s were assigned a most unusual mission to fly to Batchelor Field, 60 miles south of Darwin on the north coast of Australia, to carry out bombing missions on Dili, capital of East Timor, 477 air miles from Darwin across the Timor Sea.

The Japanese invaded Timor 20 February 1942 and defenders withdrew to the mountainous interior of the island. Two colonial powers shared the island: the Dutch in West Timor and the Portuguese in East Timor. The Timor Campaign had little strategic importance but there was one huge tactical benefit. A handful of Allied fighters were able to harass and hold a complete Japanese Infantry Division in Timor and prevent it from reinforcing the battle in New Guinea. The Australian "second-second Independent Company" later recognized as 2/2 Commando Squadron was one of 12 Australia's original commando units. The larger force in defense of Timor was code named *Sparrow.* Unfortunately 2/2 became separated and was ill-equipped with no radio to communicate.

After three months with no word they were considered dead. Living off the land with the help of friendly Timorese, who provided food, shelter, Timor ponies and guides they continued to raid and ambush the enemy. They shot-up a town to obtain a car generator and battery; with the expertise of Joe Loveless, a Tasmanian amateur radio hobbyist, they cobbled together a radio. Suddenly out of the either after five months, a signal is heard from 2/2. The Darwin listening post was suspicious; it could be a Japanese trick; to prove identity they asked, "What is Jack Sergeant's wife's Christian name?" Jack was well known by members of *Sparrow*. The response, the word JOAN, sent cheers and started a series of successful supply air-drops and earned the admiration of the nation. Meanwhile, the frustrated Japanese mounted a thrust from Dili to capture the scattered Allied unconventional guerrilla forces and ordered the capture of all Portuguese present on the island. Until then they had recognized Portugal neutrality and the presence of citizens was tolerated.

The Allied High Command authorized B-26 bombing raids on Timor. Winging their way westward across northern Australia on 31 October 1942, eight B-26s from the 2nd and 18th Bomb Squadrons, led by Major Anderson, left **Reid River** near Townsville – destination Batchelor Field, half a continent away, 1147 miles. About the same time four B-26s of the 19th and 33rd Bomb Squadrons, led by Captain Frank Allen, at **Iron Ridge** near the north tip of Cape York Peninsula, left to join the others at Batchelor Field. A direct air route for them to fly would have carried them over the Gulf of Carpentaria – that large bite in the northern landmass of Australia measuring 367 miles at the mouth and over 435 miles measured north and south. To avoid this over-water route Captain Allen charted a 395-mile dog-leg south to Cloncurry where they remained over-night. Next morning they proceeded 956 miles directly to Batchelor Field and arrived at noon 1 November 1942.

The first mission: 1 November 1942: Loaded with 100 and 500-pound bombs, nine ships headed for Dili. Approaching at 8,000 ft. they hit the center of town. Anti-aircraft fire was inaccurate. No fighter aircraft were encountered. Second mission: 3 November 1942 targeted the Catholic Church which was being used as a supply dump. Eight ships loaded with 100-pound demolition bombs and three 2,000-pounders bombed at 1130 hours. The aircraft spread out to make individual drops on the cathedral, docks and headquarter buildings. Direct hits were observed on all targets.

As the B-26s returned to formation the ship flown by Lt. Hitchcock; received direct ack-ack hits in the right nacelle, tearing off the landing gear and starting a fire in the engine. An enemy fighter zoomed in damaging the instrument panel and propeller on the burning engine. The aircraft slowed and lost altitude. With the starboard engine out, generator power was diminished; nevertheless .50-caliber turret guns remained operable and gunners reported downing two attacking Oscars. The formation continued toward Darwin. Lt. Thompson, Captain Allen's co-pilot, saw a lone Oscar flying parallel to their plane. The pilot had the canopy open and was taking pictures, Allen's turret gunner spotted him and opened fire the Oscar spiraled away and Allen's gunner was given credit for a "kill."

Meanwhile, Hitchcock's crippled Marauder leaving the island came out over the water at about 500 ft. still under attack. Lead pilot, Lt. Michaelis, wheeled his flight back to help defend Hitchcock and the attacking Oscars promptly fled. A single plane remained to escort its damaged mate. The rest, low on fuel, sped home to Darwin. On one engine the airspeed was only 135 mph and they were unable to climb. After 2 hours of flight at 1,000 ft. altitude the struggling good engine froze. "Prepare to ditch!" the plane touched the water, skimmed about 100 yards and began to settle. With cockpit overhead hatches open, Hitchcock, who had left his seat belt open, was catapulted out unhurt into the water; he climbed onto the wing and counted five of the other six crew members in the water. Still missing was Sgt. Campbell, turret gunner. Hitchcock dove down and managed to get Campbell's limp body out of the turret and into the hands of the crew. He re-entered the rapidly sinking plane and released the life-raft. The plane sank nose first in little over a minute. The escorting B-26, circling overhead, dropped a raft and first aid kit, the raft was damaged; running low on fuel it departed for Darwin. Sadly Sgt. Campbell died from a broken neck; they wrapped him in a parachute, said a prayer and buried him at sea. Two hours later a B-26 returned to drop supplies without success. Two RAAF Lockheed Hudsons appeared and dropped water, food and first-aid gear wrapped in a Mae West, as well as a large six-man raft. Accompanying the drop was a note saying that a rescue boat would pick them up the next morning at 0600 hours. Right on time, after 15 hours floating through a restless night fending off curious sharks, the Australian Navy tugboat, the *Forceful,* approached through the misty morning air, picked them up, and returned them safely to shore. On 5 November 1942, the 22nd BG flew their third and final mission against Timor.

The attack was on troop concentrations 10 miles south of Dili. Captain Allen led three planes from the 19th BS and Captain McClaran led three planes from the 2nd BS. They blanketed the target area with 100- and 500-pound bombs. The strike was completely unopposed. The B-26s were released to return to their home bases. For them the Battle of Timor was over.

By the end of 1942 the chances of the Allies re-taking Timor were remote. In December, the remainder of the original, *Sparrow* force – except for a few officers – were evacuated. Unconventional guerrilla warfare wound down. On 10 January 1943, 50 Portuguese citizens and remaining commandos were evacuated by the destroyer *HMAS Arunta.* A small intelligence team was left behind but their presence was soon detected by the Japanese. They made their way to the eastern tip of Timor where the American submarine *USS Gudgeon* picked them up. They were the last to leave, evacuated 10 February 1943. Timor remained under Japanese control until the surrender, 5 September 1945.

Chapter Fourteen

Other Torpedo Runs

Alaska – Aleutians: "The northern lights have seen strange sights but the strangest they ever did see was . . . " Those words by poet Robert Service in his book *Songs of the Sourdough,* easily describes three B-26s sitting in a snow-covered meadow with a dozen forlorn crew members "camping" under a crumpled wing waiting to be rescued. Robert Service might also have described the scene poetically by paraphrasing his poem – *The Shooting of Dangerous Dan McGrew* – "the boys were whooping it up in the Malamute saloon with the Lady known as Lou." Well, this was no saloon, there was no lady, but the boys did whoop it up when rescued. Ironically, lines from his "The Law of the Yukon" also apply: "The strong shall thrive – only the fit survive." Fortunately the stranded B-26 crew members were *fit* and the ill-fated ships were stocked with Arctic *survival* gear. Here is their story:

The three B-26s were flying the 944-mile leg, from Edmonton, Alberta, Canada to Whitehorse in the Yukon Territory on their way to Elmendorf Field, Fairbanks, Alaska. This was the route for ferrying airplanes to Alaska and for sending lend-lease planes onward to Russia. These three B-26s would be part of the 77th Bombardment Squadron, 28th Composite Group destined for duty in the Aleutian Island chain. A Lt. Doolittle (no relation to Jimmy) led this flight.

Navigating with homemade maps, no navigation aids, no

beacons, on Friday, 16 January 1942, a day short on daylight; they were battling snow squalls, low visibility over uncharted territory with a gas gauge bouncing on zero – they were lost – a controlled crash-landing was their only survival option. An open meadow with no trees looked promising. Five foot snow-covered bushes cushioned their slide. They were down with only two injuries. Co-pilot Lt. Howard Smiley tells what happened. "At the same time we were enroute to Alaska a flight of P-40s was also enroute, they were one day behind us having stopped at Fort Nelson, B. C.

When we were reported missing they delayed departure and searched for us for several days. They were ordered to continue to Watson Lake their next stop. Fortunately for us, we had crashed about 90 miles from Watson Lake but 30 miles off the proper flight path. On the day that these P-40s and their accompanying C-47 spotted us it was clear, cold and still. You could hear for miles it seemed. We were in the shelter when all of a sudden we heard this low humming sound; we looked outside. There in the distance were four little dots almost hidden by treetops. Our crew had prepared for this so we let fly with flares and gun tracers – a real 4th of July display. Then we waited. I will never forget the tremendous thrill as those four little dots turned toward us and flew over us. We were no longer lost! Success! The missing bombers were found! Elmendorf Field and the RCMP "Mounties" were alerted. On the next day two bush pilots flying an old high-wing single engine ski-equipped Fokker landed nearby. Their passenger was a RCMP constable. The pilots flew the two injured pilots to Watson Lake. The constable stayed with us and led us to a frozen lake 5 or 6 miles away where we cleared a makeshift runway and in about a week were flown out by a ski-equipped C-47. Army technicians stripped the planes of motors and useful gear, abandoning the fuselage and wings to the elements.

The site was forgotten until 1971 when airplane collector David Tallichet, intrigued by bush-pilot stories, discovered the valuable wrecks and started the costly recovery – newspapers called it "The

Million Dollar Valley." – Of the 5,266 total Martin B-26 Marauders built fewer than 6 are preserved in museums and only one, assembled from these three relics, is flyable. It can be seen at Kermit Weeks – Fantasy of Flight collection, in Polk City, Florida. Meanwhile, we return to 1942 and the 77th Bomb Squadron story. It is said the 77th BS was the first B-26 outfit to leave the states, "for foreign-land duty."

Early in 1942 the 77th BS staged in Boise, Idaho where the field commander was Major "Light Horse Harry" Wilson star half-back for Army West Point class of 1928. Another future recognizable enlisted airman's name, but not yet a movie star, was Charlton Heston. Geographically, the Aleutians are strung out southwestward, like stepping stones forming a short-cut to Tokyo. Admiral Yamamoto's attack on Dutch Harbor, 4 June 1942, timed to coincide with the attack on Midway, would also protect Japan's northern flank. As part of the plan the Japanese invaded and held Kiska and Attu until August 1943. When American troops retook these islands they found the islands had been abandoned. On 3 June 1942 a Japanese task force was reported in the North Pacific.

The 77th BS had been deployed to Umnak Island's, Fort Glenn Army airstrip made of PSP (Pierced Steel Planking). "It was a sea of mud," wrote Lt. Bailey K. Howard, Squadron Historian, "we had to pitch our tents and crews cooked their own food." Lt. Howard's well-compiled *History of the 77th BS (Medium), Attu, Alaska, authorized CG, 11th AF, is dated 16 June 1944.* Only a typed copy is available; it may not have been formally published. It covers the period 15 January 1941 to 31 December 1943, Major Robert S. Hamey, Squadron CO. Report Section III, titled Missions and Accomplishments, includes data from Operations Summary, 29 May through 6 June 1942 and an award authorization – General Order Number 68 Hdq ADC, Fort Richardson, Alaska, 1 August 1942. Lt. Howard relied on numerous sources to substantiate his narrative. We quote his entry:

"On the morning of 3 June 1942 a Japanese Task Force was reported approaching Dutch Harbor. A flight of 6 B-26s went on search. No contact was made, and Captain Meals made a belly landing at Umnak; but no injuries were sustained. On the morning of 4 June 1942 the Japanese attacked Dutch Harbor, and we sent four B-26s to intercept; no contact was made. The second flight of five B-26s was sent out to intercept, leaving Umnak at 2050W, and Captain Meals and Lt. Northamer made contact and sunk a Japanese heavy cruiser with a direct torpedo hit. As a result of this action, Captain Meals was decorated with the Distinguished Service Cross, and Lt. Northamer the Distinguished Flying Cross. The weather during the entire period of 29 May to 6 June was practically prohibitive for flying. No weather information west of Unmak was available. The weather was marked by rain and fog. On returning from 4 June mission's planes flew for four hours over water at 50 feet altitude or less in fog. On landing, the far end of the runway could not be seen. During this period the danger of attack from the enemy by carrier based planes was a real hazard. On 4 June Umnak Field was attacked in the morning by four dive bombers and in the afternoon by nine Zero pursuit planes making strafing attacks. No planes or personnel were hit." Meanwhile, in another war zone, 5,800 miles south from the Bering Sea to the Coral Sea, B-26s of the 69th BS are stationed at:

New Caledonia –"Poppy": "In Flanders field the poppies blow," the key word, selected by an anonymous code-maker, was "Poppy." Henceforth, this word from Dr. John McCrae's World War One battlefield poem would be the codename for the French possession in the Coral Sea – "Poppy" – New Caledonia. We ask, was it the whim of a history buff or was it the studied tactful recognition of French sensibilities – a symbol of remembrance – a boutonniere of good Franco – American relationships of the past? We hope it was the latter because an avalanche named, "Poppy Force" – the 23rd Infantry "Americal" Division (Task Force 6184) was about to descend on Noumea, Capital of New Caledonia, "L-day" – landing day – was 13 March 1942.

A week after Major General Alexander Patch's Infantry came ashore; there was another "Landing Day" 19 March 1942. The first B-26 of the 22nd Bombardment Group touched down and got stuck in the mud at Plaines des Gaiacs. (See Chapter 7 for details.) For the 22nd BG, New Caledonia was merely a refueling stop on the way to Brisbane, Australia and future combat in the skies of New Guinea and Rabaul, New Britain. Other B-26 Groups were in the trans-Pacific pipeline. On 13 June the 69th BS departed Hickam Field, Hawaii and arrived 23 June at Tontouta Airfield, Noumea, New Caledonia, where they remained over-night (RON) and then on, 24 June, flew 120 miles north to the new airfield, Plaine des Gaiacs, their new home. By now, three months since being stuck in the mud, the runway was serviceable but other amenities were incomplete and the water supply was two miles from the airfield.

New Caledonia is in a key geographical position, Noumea south to Auckland, New Zealand, is 1,125 air-miles; to the north, 987 air-miles, is Guadalcanal. It became a major support base under direct control of the War Department. The 69th BS, detached from the 38th BG operated independently under the leadership of Colonel Rich as directed by COMAIRSOPAC, Rear Admiral John "Slew" McCain. On 26 June they made their first patrol over the Coral Sea. On 1 July they received a sub-alert and found it was only a whale. On two occasions 6 July and 11 July, 12 planes armed with bombs and torpedoes responded to a report of an approaching Japanese fleet. It was a "no-show" each time. Torpedo training continued. On 15 July nine B-26s were practicing torpedo runs with destroyer *USS MacFarland* when a Japanese sub suddenly surfaced in their practice area; it made a crash-dive but it was too late. The B-26s dropped bombs, the destroyer released depth charges. Wreckage was observed, the 69thBS was credited with an "assist."

The 69th BS participated in a variety of activities like escorting P-39s and F4Fs to outlying islands, searching for lost aircraft and dropping emergency supplies to stranded airmen. On 5 September,

Major General Millard F. Harmon, Commanding General Air Force South Pacific Area, Major General Alexander Patch, Army, New Caledonia and Colonel Rich, CO 69th BS participated in the ceremony awarding the DSC to Captain Collins for his action at the Battle of Midway. (See Cover Story) On 17 October General "Hap" Arnold visited Plaines des Gaiacs.

Torpedo training for B-26 crews convened at Nowra, Australia. (see Chapter 11 Nowra) After two B-26 squadrons were trained the program was closed. The 22nd BG no longer carried torpedoes in their arsenal. The 69th BS continued patrols with less emphasis on torpedo launching. By spring 1943, B-26 aircraft were phased out and squadrons with B-25 aircraft were perfecting "skip-bombing." The only successful sinking of an enemy vessel by a torpedo launched from a B-26 was accomplished on, 4 June 1942, in the Aleutians. Hence forth, **Army's Torpedo Challenge – faded away.**

Epilogue

The Airplane: On 25 November 1940. Number 40-1361 in tests Top Speed was 315 mph at 15,000 ft. Maximum Range 675 miles without auxiliary fuel tanks. Cruising speed 282 mph. Ceiling 23,507 ft. (4.45 miles high) First purchase by USAAF 201 airplanes – by the end of production 5,266 were built. The first 4 were assigned to the 22nd BG at Langley Field, Virginia.

The 22nd Bombardment Group (Medium): Was formed 22 December 1939 at Mitchell Field New York. It was activated 1 February 1940 and moved to Langley Field, Virginia, 14 November 1940. The Group included the following Squadrons: 2nd BS activated 1 February 1940 at Bolling Field, moved to Langley 14 November 1940; 19th BS activated 1 February 1940 at Patterson Field, OH, moved to Langley 16 November 1940; 33rd BS activated 1 February 1940 at Patterson Field, OH, moved to Langley 16 November 1940; 18th Recon. Squadron activated Mitchell Field 1 September 1936, moved to Langley 15 November 1940. Before receiving B-26s they flew B-18s, a derivative of the Douglas DC-2. On 22 February 1941 the USAAF accepted the B-26 and the first four were assigned to Langley Field. By 21 April 1941 the 22BG received its full complement of 54 aircraft (13 per Squadron). Other records list 60 B-26s at Langley.

War Operations: The 22nd Bombardment Group was the first complete air group sent by the U.S. into a combat theater. During the first nine months of combat, 5 April 1942 – 11 January 1943, the 22nd BG established the following record:

147 Combat missions flown; 94 enemy fighters were claimed shot down; 6 B-26s lost to enemy fighters; 14 shot down by anti-aircraft guns; 7 lost on the ground by enemy action; 37 lost due to mechanical failure, accidents, weather and lack of fuel.

Total airplane sorties flown: 841; destruction by the enemy in the air: 20 airplanes. The loss percentage of 2.38 was the heaviest of any B-26 Group as of January 1943. Please Note: In the ETO (European Theater of Operations) the loss rate of .5 of 1% was the lowest combat loss rate of any World War Two aircraft

Sadly the number of crew members lost was 114 by all causes.

When recalled from battle only 16 B-26 airplanes remained. The 22nd "Red Raiders" BG, with new personnel switched to B-25 Mitchell Medium bombers and later to B-24 Heavy bombers.

Writer Martin Cardin wrote: The B-26 was bold, clean, swift and deadly.

Barnstorming Pilots: Buzzing down an enemy aircraft carrier's flight deck was not a stunt – it was survival! However, a dog and pony show using live ammunition and bombs, was a stunt of sorts, staged by Pentagon impresarios to convince skeptical "ground-pounders" that tactical airpower carried a punch. Captain Allen has been reassigned and joins an Air Corps armada of: 20 B-26s, 26 A-20s and 40 assorted P-39s, P-40s to put on a demonstration maneuver between 18 January 1944 and 13 February 1944 performing for thousands of troops at: Fort Benning, GA; Fort Sill, OK; Fort Knox, KY and Atterbury, IN, Infantry Division Training Ground then back to Hinter Field, Savannah, GA; where he was promoted. Major Allen comments, "We impressed the hell out of 10,000 Infantry Officers." Unfortunately the maneuver was not without bad luck. For some unknown treason a B-26 spun-in over Arkansas. Allen writes home that his Paratrooper boots picked up at Fort Benning, "Are nearly broken in."

Hunter Field is a staging airfield for receiving brand new B-26s, calibrating compasses and instruments and flying fuel consumption test flights. The new 397th Bomb Group is getting their planes in commission. The crews had trained together when the Group formed in Tampa, FL three months earlier. This was their POM – Preparing for Overseas Movement – and the inspection team was not merciful. Major Allen is the 598th Squadron Commander. He wrote, "Crews are improving techniques; my Squadron got through inspection OK, but Group didn't do too well." Administrative chores are ironed out. He writes, "I got Major Majors to straighten up my Per Diem orders." Yes, shades of characters in the novel, "Catch 22." The Administrative Officer's real name is Majors. We also had a Chaplain, Captain Comfort. Note: I said "we", it was my good luck, months later, to be the first replacement Bombardier reporting to Lt. Col. Frank Allen's, 598th BS at Rivenhall Airdrome in England in mid July 1944; that is an exciting tale for another time.

B-26 Marauder Memorial Guide: The original book with pictures and location information was compiled by Al E. Baxter, member of the Washington Area Marauder Men (WAMM) chapter of the B-26 Marauder Historical Society (MHS) published 8 May 1995. Al added changes and content in a second edition in September 2015. These versions were written primarily for Marauder men references. The next revision by Marshall Magruder, September 2016, with photographs and new information included a new format as a helpful guidebook enabling individuals unable to visit the monuments and memorials to see and read inscriptions and has links for additional internet information, if available. The 2016 edition has three parts, Part One lists memorials within the continental U.S. (approx. 200 pages); Part Two lists memorials outside the U.S. (approx. 200 pages). Part Three contains information about Marauder men who were killed in action (KIA) and about those missing in action (MIA), arranged by cemeteries under American Battle Monument Commission administration. These are listed numerically by bombardment group and squadron designation. There is also a summary table of numbers of KIA/MIA airmen from each bomb group/squadron. The 2016 edition is available in color or B&W printed version also as a CD-ROM disk from the B-26 Marauder Historical Society, 3900 E. Timrod St. Tucson, AZ 85711.

The Greatest Generation – Roll Out: On Tuesday 4 April 1944, the last of 1,585 B-26 Marauders rolled out of the Martin, Nebraska assembly plant. It was a moment of pride and celebration. Production of the Marauder had tapered off to allow for gradual retooling and assembly of another legendary warplane, the B-29. Dedicated Martin-Marauder people remained on the job bolstered by the memory of their winning production prizes while making their "first love" the sleek B-26. For the B-29, the vast assembly floor was expanded. In the fall of 1944 engineers were told to install a modification on selected B-29s enabling them to carry a special heavy bomb. Col. Paul W. Tibbetts, Jr., pilot of the *Enola Gay,* brought a reasonable copy of the real thing for trial installation. It worked and the Omaha plant produced over 20 of the specially designed bombers. Seven decades have pasted and the "Greatest Generation of Marauder Men" are still "Rolling Out". . . . a thin blue "First Gen." line, to be sure, but **MHS (Marauder Historical Society),** has a plan to extend the legend. With your membership they stand ready to carry the story of the plane and its people forward.

Airplane Affection: In the grim environment of war young aviators form a special light-hearted attachment to their vehicle, their airplane, "she" becomes animate. Merrill's quotation says it all: "I flew in old 40-1549 *'Bluegrass Bettye'* today – beat-up as she is, she really hopped off the ground – showing off for me – 'cause she used to be my plane and it's the first time I've ridden in her for months." We see that *Bettye's* nose art and Merrill's imagination has created a mix of loyalty and fondness; "she's" more than a machine. Paraphrasing General Kenney's remark says it best, "The B-26 takes care of you and brings you home."

Stan Walsh: Editor-in-Chief, Author. 1st Lt. Bombardier, Stan joined "Chief", Lt. Col. Frank Allen's 598th Squadron, 397th Bomb Group, 9th Air Force Bombardment Division in 1944 and completed 65 combat missions over enemy held Europe. In the 1930s his young eyes were on the sky watching the Navy dirigible *USS Akron* and German zeppelin *Hindenburg* maneuver over the pine forests of New Jersey. A 1951 graduate of the University of Southern California, with a Civil Engineering degree his career included planning and construction of Dulles Int'l Airport in Virginia and aviation oriented projects in Asia, Latin America, North Africa and Europe. A photographic hobby turned into a second career, he produced documentary film lecture programs ranging from the Andes to the Alps including: Bolivia; the Philippine Islands; Italy's Lakes; Spain; Sicily; French Riviera and Corsica. Previous publication was **First Over the Front,** letters from France during World War One by Lt. "Billy" Schauffler, pilot First Aero Squadron and friend of the other "Billy", General William Mitchell. They learned to fly together in 1916-17. Stan is a Member Emeritus of the Explorers Club. He is at home in Rancho Palos Verdes, California.

Jack Fellows – Aviation Artist: A commercial and fine art painter for over 35 years, Jack is the foremost artist in the world documenting the Pacific WW II period aviation art. His work is widely collected by museums and private collectors. He is a member of the USAF Art Program. His focus on the history of air war in the Pacific led to originating the "*Cactus Air Force*" Art Project; this informal designation applies to aviators flying off of captured Henderson Field, on Guadalcanal in support of marines and troops battling to secure the island. Jack was President of the American Society of Aviation

Artists, 1995-97. He is a guest lecturer at the Museum of Flight, Seattle. Jack has approximately one-hundred postage-stamp designs to his credit. His honors include the R.G. Smith Award for *Excellence in Naval Aviation Art*. Original art, limited edition Prints, Sketches and Books are available through JackFellows.com.

Col. Frank Allen's daughter, Jeanne Allen Newell and brother Ralph Allen enjoy a sea story with Captain Peter Walsh at the B-26 banquet, 2017, celebrating the 75th anniversary of the Battle of Midway, 4 June 1942.

Jenn Merritt, MHS Executive Secretary, displays "Marauders Always Attack" blanket, a special "silent auction" prize at a recent B-26 veterans' reunion.

Brian Gibbons, dedicated B-26 Marauder archivist, adds clarification to a caller's inquiry; "Yes Sir, it's a long story; here's what really happened." . . . Brian and Karla Gibbons pursue elusive Marauder facts like a Spitfire chasing a wayward "Buzz-bomb." For answers the buzz-word is "Go to Brian"; we're glad he brought his "Sherlock Holmes" search talent to US from merry 'ole England.

The B-26 Goes to War, Co-author and Editor-in-chief: Stan Walsh. The model B-26 carries special black & white Normandy invasion stripes. A top secret project kept thousands of buckets of paint and bushels of brushes in limbo awaiting the cryptic order – "You may Paint" – flashed to all squadrons shortly before D-Day, 6 June 1944. Stripes were hurriedly applied to aircraft to help trigger-happy gunners, on battleships and beaches, to quickly identify friendly aircraft.

B-26 Marauder granite monument in Memorial Park, National Museum of the United States Air Force, Wright Paterson Air Force Base, Fairfield Ohio, near Dayton.

Marauder-men and family members place a memorial wreath at the Air Force Memorial on a hill overlooking Washington DC during their reunion, June 2017.

United States Air Force Memorial – Washington DC – June 2017 – "Oh, I have slipped the surly bonds of earth . . . put out my hand and touched the face of God." These lines are from the poem "High Flight" by John Gillespie Magee, (June 1922-December 1941) an American pilot officer with the Royal Canadian Air Force – poem used courtesy of the United States Air Force.

Appendix A

History 101

To understand what happens when a nation is ill-prepared and woefully outmatched in military matters let's brush up on what happened in Europe during 1938-1939. The prelude to World War Two.

On March 12, 1938, Austria was annexed by Germany into Hitler's *Anschluss* – "Uniting all German speaking people," he said. The Austrian Army, to avoid bloodshed, was told to "stand down." The Allies did not oppose the take-over although it was a clear violation of the Versailles Treaty; they had no way to enforce it. In Vienna cheering crows welcomed the *Wehrmacht* with flags and flowers. Reporters called it the *Blumenkrieg*, "War of Flowers."

Across the channel English gardens were in full bloom. Tea and cucumber sandwiches were served during springtime Cricket matches. At London's famous Royal Chelsea Flower Show rival flower growers engaged in a friendly – 'bloomin' *Blumenkreig*. But wait! High above it all – at *Berchtesgarden* – *Hitlers's Eagle's Nest, in Bavaria* –Hitler was not growing posies. He had his eye on Czechoslovakia and boldly announced his intent to annex and set October 1, 1938, as the deadline for doing it. War jitters swept Europe. Shuttle diplomacy started in earnest. Using British Airways Lockheed Electra model 14, an upgrade of model 10, the plane flown by Amelia Earhart, British Prime Minister Neville Chamberlain met German Chancellor Adolf Hitler who agreed to "talk things over" in Munich.

The big four of Europe – Hitler, Mussolini, Daladier and Chamberlain, (Germany, Italy, France, Great Britain) – met on September 29. They agreed, without asking, Czechoslovakia, *"by your leave, may we cede German speaking Sudetenland to Herr Hitler?"* They did it without batting an eye and called it "Peace with Honor." Chamberlain hurried home, landing at London's Heston Airdrome on September 30. Waving a piece of paper, the Munich Agreement, as he deplaned, newsreel cameras captured the inspired speech, "Peace in our time!" he shouted. At Number 10 Downing Street, crowds sang, "He's a jolly good fellow" – out of tune, because – six months later, March 1939, Herr Hitler gobbled up the rest of Czechoslovakia.

English gardens bloomed again in 1939, but it was the last peaceful summer Europe would know for six long years. On September 1, 1939 Hitler invaded Poland, and the walls came tumbling down. Two days later Britain declared war on Germany. For six months the Western Front remained silent. The French called it *Drole de guerre – the Phony War* – Suddenly, during the first wartime spring, May 10, 1940, German Divisions *blitzed* through Dutch tulip fields and the Ardennes (a name we'll see again – Battle of the Bulge). British troops, "Advancing to the rear," reached Dunkirk and were heroically rescued, May 26 – June 4. The new Prime Minister, Winston Churchill, on May 13, 1940, offered the nation ". . . Blood, toil, tears and sweat . . . never surrender." In America, newly commissioned, Lt. Frank S. Allen, military aviator with silver wings, reported for active duty at Mitchell Field, Long Island, NY. History Lesson 101 – complete – class dismissed.

Appendix B

Code Breakers

Air attacks on Pearl Harbor had been a standard scenario in annual fleet exercises' since 1928. General Billy Mitchell had warned of such an attack in a detailed report as early as 1927. But, of course, that was only make-believe. How do we know when to plan ahead for the real thing ?

In 1940, US code-breakers had broken the Japanese diplomatic code. While not containing much military information this new data helped paint the "big picture" of Japanese intentions. A new descriptive code name was needed. The words "Red" and "Blue" had already been used to label earlier break-through; the code-breakers reasoned, this new information on their "artful espionage" palette would blend nicely like two artists' pigments, red and blue creating a third color – being artists of sort – they cleverly called the mix "Code Purple." Intercepts from this new secret source were simply called "Magic." These messages were read only by a few high officials in Washington DC; copies were never made.

Meanwhile at Pearl Harbor Navy code breakers succeeded in

breaking the Imperial Japanese Navy General Operational Code which they labeled JN-25b. This was crucial to our success at the Battle of Midway. It was Admiral Nimitz' "Ace in the hole." The brooding hostile attitude of Japan toward the US because of trade embargos was common knowledge and the on-going war in Europe cast a long, anxious shadow so preparedness was on everyone's mind. On August 27, 1940 the National Guard was federalized for short-term training, *"A Year and a Day"* became their "tag-line."

Newspaper editors also had their marketing "tag-lines" reminding reporters – *"Headlines Sell Papers."* Following a routine interview with Lt. Gen. Walter C. Short, Commanding General, Army Hawaiian Department, on August 14, 1941, the prominent newspaper *Honolulu Advertiser* headline read: "General Short Sees Danger of Oahu Air Raid." Two weeks later on Sunday, November 30th the headline read, "Japan May Strike Over Weekend". In a follow-up edition on Friday, December 5th it was, "Pacific Zero Hour Near." Reporters had no special access to secret codes; they were merely guessing. Using their fertile imaginations they might also have seen a "phantom" newsroom "War-Clock" and noticed it ominously ticking away in strange unison with *real* "War-Clocks" in wardrooms of the Imperial Japanese fleet – counting down the hours to 0755 AM Sunday morning. To readers of the *Honolulu Advertiser these* scary headlines were boring – old news. Reporters were passing time speculating on a slow-news day. They had finished their work, covered their typewriters, turned out the lights, retreated to a favorite watering hole, ordered a double and mused, "How do I spend a dull weekend?" – Sunday, December 7th – Their rhetorical question got a shocking answer – bombs fell – reeling in disbelief reporters, editors, typesetters, pressmen, song-writers raced to their keyboards and typewriters. They quickly forged new headlines – new tunes to tell the story – a new "tag-line" – became a slogan that rallied a stunned nation – ***"Let's Remember Pearl Harbor."***

Editor's note: Let's review the training 1st Lt. Allen and other pilots of the 22nd Bombardment Group must undergo to prepare for operational flying.

Appendix C

Patterson Field – Pilot Check-Out

Patterson Field, Fairfield, Ohio near Dayton: Lt. Allen writes: "I flew from the left seat today." He is being "checked-out," learning to fly the B-26 with "Bum," his classmate Lt. Bumgardener. They are learning all about the new medium (M) bomber. On February 22, 1941, the first four aircraft off the Martin production line were delivered to the 22 BG 19 Squadron, Langley Field, Virginia. It is destined to be the first B-26 combat group so all the pilots are here at Patterson learning about its idiosyncrasies – "which seems to be many," says Frank.

In letters to his wife Jeanne, Frank writes: August 8, 1941: Lt. McCutcheon had an engine cut out on him this afternoon, then the other went partly out and he arrived in a corn patch. Didn't get hurt although the underside of the airplane is pretty torn up. I was flying when it happened so we flew around and found the scene about three miles from the field. After that accident all B-26s were grounded until they have been inspected. All the rush of the three past days is now completely reversed. We're grounded until tomorrow. The

"Hotel Fado," (Fairfield Air Depot) my address on the field, is not a hotel at all but is a large room between two immense hangars where they keep our planes and work on them at night. There are 50 of us, mostly B-26 pilots but a few P-40 folks.

"Hooray! I've been given my final check and spent the rest of the morning flying around with a new co-pilot. A violent thunderstorm came up and I rushed back to the field and just did get in ahead of it before it hit the field. Several former classmates came in for transition training and it seemed almost like we were back at the flying school. They brag about flying hot pursuits but backed-off when learning I'm flying the really "hot" one.

"My first real 'kick' out of flying came when I flew a Boeing P-12F shortly after graduating from Kelly. The P-12F is a 1932 modification of the 1928 biplane first used by the Navy. With 500HP it had a ceiling of 31,000ft. It was the last biplane flown by Army and Navy. My next big 'kick' came out of flying the B-26, and yet I had another. I got to fly a P-39 the Bell Air Cobra which recently did 675 mph in a dive. I had a late model, guns, cannon through the nose 'n everything. It had a late model Allison engine only good for 1,150 horses. The takeoff was so sensational that I forgot to pull up the wheels until I was about 1,000 feet in the air. I pulled them up and the next thing I knew I was at 5,000 feet. I pushed the nose down a little and immediately I was back at 1,000 feet doing better than 400 mph. The first time I've been over 400 mph. I horsed back to gain maximum climb and in about 20 seconds I was back at 5,000 feet again. What an airplane! After about an hour of tearing around I came in and landed. It landed like a charm. One of the easiest ships to land that I've had in quite awhile. It came in hot but it was easy to handle and had nice landing characteristics. Now, if they can get the Lockheed P-38, in shape before I leave, it's been promised to me. From a 300 mph bomber to a 400 mph pursuit ship in a week. Some fun!

August 17, 1941: A colonel came in from Washington DC

and gave us the dope. We'll all stay here until the service tests are completed and every pilot has 50 hours on the ship and then – provided the maneuvers were still on, we'll go to them. But not before the planes are ready. Waiting for the "bugs" to be worked out in the airplane and not flying is boring. Housing is scarce, he wrote, so Jeanne did not join Frank at Fairfield. There was talk of returning to wait at Langley but that didn't happen. The planes are finally ready but it is raining so no flying. To fill the time we had a lecture by Lt. Olson on how to compute C.G. (Center of Gravity). It left the boys more confused than they were before. Flying resumed and by Mid September the pilots had acquired 50 hours in the B-26 and were cleared to go to the Louisiana Maneuvers.

Editor's note: Louisiana Maneuvers, September 1941, were to test men and equipment for war. Troops had trained here during World War One and it was still sparsely populated. Lt. Allen is there. Join him in: Appendix D

Appendix D

Louisiana Maneuvers

"There were soldiers everywhere," said a Louisiana farmer. "It was the Battle of the Bayous," wrote a newspaper editor. In fact it was the greatest sham battle in U.S. history – a practice for war that had already started in Europe.

Nearly half a million men and their equipment participated between September 12, 1941 and September 29th. The Army Air Forces gained autonomy (on June 20 Air Corps became Air Forces) and Major General H.H. "Hap" Arnold assigned two medium bomber groups, B-26 and B-25 plus P-39 and P-40 squadrons to participate. The maneuvers were to become a proving ground for tanks and airplanes. Light non-combative airplanes, like the Piper Cub, L-4, dubbed "Grasshoppers" were introduced by Major Richard T. Coiner and proved to be popular and very successful. Colonel Coiner later commanded the 397 BG, (B-26s) in Europe.

The maneuvers had two phases, prior to the second phase a bombing demonstration was arranged at Barksdale Field. On September 23rd the *NY Times* reported, "Bombers Thrill War Games

Troops." Radio commentators, Eric Severide and Drew Pearson, when describing the "games" told how Lt. Col. Dwight D. Eisenhower and Lt. Col. George S. Patton had executed a daring *blitzkrieg* dash. The entire 2nd Armored Division advanced 200 miles in 3 days to envelope an "enemy" army. When the "enemy" General complained that Patton went outside the rules of the war-game doing an end-run via East Texas, irrepressible George Patton responded, "I am unaware of such rules in war." The umpires agreed, "It was a brilliant move," and they ended the mock "War."

General George C. Marshall, Chief of Staff, kept a little black book noting names of junior officers that exhibited vision, resourcefulness and progressive ideas. Ike and Patton were added as was Mark Clark, Omar Bradley and "Vinegar" Joe Stilwell. We know the story. Eight days after Pearl Harbor Ike was called to Washington, promoted to Brigadier General and shortly thereafter went to London to plan Operation Torch, the invasion of North Africa.

Let's return to 1st Lt. Frank Allen on his way to the Louisiana "Hayride" Maneuvers. Camping in tents on the flight line under simulated war conditions with pounding rain and the threat of a hurricane was anything but a tuneful "hayride."

September 12, 1941: We arrived at Ellington Field near Houston, Texas at 6:00PM after stopping at Barksdale to check the weather and get a new clearance. I got here just in time for supper. According to Captain Mudheiser, our operations officer, we should be back at Langley by the end of the month and it is doubtful we'll go on the Carolina maneuvers. We're living in tents along the ramp and we must stay in the vicinity constantly. The "War" starts Sunday night. From then on we go on "air alert" which means we must be ready to leave 5 minutes after we receive orders. The town, Houston, is 20 miles away; it's a small world. Would you believe, Bud Colegrove, who was my bosom companion through grammar school and my first year in high school, is the Army and Navy editor of the Houston Press?

September 14, 1941: I ran a B-26 off the concrete runway yesterday morning and one wheel sank into the mud about two feet; it took all morning to get it out. I was in disfavor for a while and had to buy beer for the B-26 guys. Now my damned airplane has a flat tire. Nuts! General Krogstad got news of an approaching hurricane that might hit here so he had everyone take down their tents and move their stuff into barracks. The storm never arrived so now we're putting the tents up again and Major Lewis is sore, as is everyone else, wondering if this was just part of the "war game?" It's hotter 'n blue blazes down here and the humidity is extremely high. We go around in our flying suits constantly dripping. Michaelis is drinking a coke and stating, "I'd like to pour it over my head."

Wow! What a time! Last night, September 15, the hardest rain I have ever seen started coming down and didn't let up until late this morning, the 16th. Our tent got full of water and after it mixed with this lousy east Texas dirt it made the gummiest mess you have ever seen. Fortunately they gave us hip boot; the mud is about a foot deep. When the weather cleared a mission was ordered out. They had to return about an hour out due to bad weather toward Shreveport. My plane is still grounded because I haven't received my oil seal from the depot. I spent the day getting my tent dug out and digging a huge drainage ditch to keep the water out. They have wooden barracks down the line but we can't use them because we are supposed to be in the field. We even have to get special permission to go to the Post Exchange.

We had special visitors; General Arnold, General Emmons and the Air Secretary of War came in but took special pains not to notice our mud piles. They drove down the ramp to look at the airplanes and now are probably comfortably ensconced in Houston. I understand that a lot of these higher officers are not sold on the B-26. They have heard wild stories like the plane will go 450 mph. Wouldn't that be a kick? Major Lewis seems to be an excellent commanding officer and one of the few who doesn't get so bound up in silly paperwork and detail that he doesn't know what's going on. As of now we haven't been able to do the "bombing" the big guns want in order to stop the Red tank advance coming down quite rapidly from Shreveport. I wish my plane part would get here. I missed the first attempted mission.

September 17, 1941: My friend Bud Colegrove with the Houston Press, came out this morning and got his ride in a B-25. They wouldn't let him ride in a B-26 as they thought it too dangerous. I wish I would have had him with me this afternoon. My part didn't come in so they gave me another plane. Our afternoon's mission was my flight of three, Warner, Macuthcheon and I were supposed to go to Jackson, Miss. where some of our "enemy" planes are and "bomb" the airport. Theoretically we had thirty 100 pound bombs in each ship. We got up there without mishap, "dropped" our bombs and started home. About 5 minute later we were attacked by 6 "enemy" P-39s. Warner was leading; he shoved up the speed a bit but not nearly as much as we would have if we were shooting real bullets. We dove down to about 50 feet above the ground and leveled off. The '39s followed us. For about 30 minutes I witnessed the damnedest exhibition of flying I've ever seen. Inasmuch as I was flying on Joe's left wing I couldn't see the guys attacking me, but the guys attacking Joe would come up over the top, not much faster than we were going, and then cut away not more than ten or fifteen feet from me and in front. All of this at about 300 miles per hour. Actually if we had had our turrets firing all of the planes that came that close would undoubtedly have been shot down by us. They were so close at times we could have hit them with slingshots without taking aim. As they passed about 30 miles faster than we I would occasionally wave. Finally they went away. According to the (war games) empires we lost one B-26; however they ruled that we shot down two of them.

In another engagement, Manson's flight "bombed" Barksdale Field and was attacked by five P-39s; he used more power than we and very successfully eluded them by excess speed and dodging into some convenient clouds. When we got back we discovered that our airport had been "bombed" so we couldn't land and had to simulate going to Dallas. Then we landed. Theoretically we "stay" in Dallas over-night and "fly back" tomorrow after the runway is "fixed." Also, remember the plane shot down, well, it now becomes the "new replacement." So much for "war games."

September 18, 1941: We had an interesting mission this afternoon. It seems that the "enemy" armored forces have broken through south of Shreveport and are in danger of surrounding and cutting off one of our large divisions. We located them this morning and bombed them. This afternoon we located them again. Instead of "bombing" we peeled off in trail dove down on the deck – tree top level – we simulate a strafing attack. Oh boy, what fun legally buzzing a long column of Infantry! Then we located a cluster of parked armored cars and put more bombs on them. Then I found a command post or the headquarters of the Red armored force. I dove down within 50 feet. All the brass hats were standing outside watching. It's a "game" so I thumbed my nose when I went by. It seemed the thing to do. Still on the deck I found a convoy of trucks and then picked up a column of armored cars. It was funny to see them swing their heavy water-cool machine guns toward us as we went down the road doing 300 mile an hour. I spotted a small airport with small observation planes. We "bombed" it as well. We didn't get picked up by any pursuit planes. I guess the umpires ruled them "out" after we bombed their airport yesterday. The "big guns' are awfully anxious to have the advance stopped and apparently the ground troops are unable to do it. We certainly gave them the works today. They were "bombed" by a total of 18 B-26s and about 27 B-25s. When we are flying, the "war's" fun but the rest of the time it is boring.

September 20, 1941: On my morning flight we started to be attacked by a flight of P-40s but were saved by a flight of Navy Grummans. I don't know where they came from but they certainly saved us. The ensuing dog fight looked even phonier than a movie one. There were planes on each other's tails all over the sky. In the meantime we discovered an entire division of 80 tanks; we bombed them and later learned the umpires ruled them destroyed and the "Army surrendered." So we have a brief rest. Poor Bud was to get another ride in a B-25 when the "War" ended."

During the October interlude the lessons learned were critiqued. In spite of unsolved problems, General Arnold said, "Concentrating aviation under one air command proved flexibility and economy of force." Before the surrender our field was bombed. One of the planes developed engine trouble so had to land. We all grabbed our pistols, ran out and made the pilot our "prisoner." I gave Bud this pretty humorous story. I hope it gets printed.

November 3, 1941: Surprise! Surprise! Its more war games this time in the Carolinas. Tanks apparently won the Louisiana "war" by moving fast. So far this "war" is a luxury one, living in barracks, eating at a mess hall, driving on paved roads. Wow! Yesterday we had time off so we went hunting. After tramping more than an hour through underbrush thick with briars and hidden swamps, we finally bagged three butterflies, one grasshopper and seven cat-n-nine tails. Lt. Allen didn't detail his flying activities in Carolina probably because they were similar to missions in Louisiana.

Two "war" game aviation innovations tested and adopted made history: Engineers, in a field near Marston, North Carolina, put down a 5,000 ft. steel runway in 72 hours. First called "Marston Mat" it worked well and became universally known as – PSP – Pierced Steel Planking. The first overseas PSP aircraft landing was on January 24, 1942 on Bluie West One (BW-1) in Greenland. The other inspiration was using "Grasshopper" airplanes. They had flown over 3,000 liaison missions during maneuvers. Each light plane cost 1/10th the price of a standard observation plane. The War Department ordered 6 to 10 such planes be assigned to every Division. They became the Ancestors of Army Aviation. The Carolina maneuvers ended and critiques began. One week after the final critique on November 30, we were at war – it was December 7th, 1941.

Appendix E

Generals and Lieutenants

"Generals and 2ⁿᵈ Lieutenants are the easiest people to work with"

In our story Captain Allen and 1ˢᵗ Lt. Dewan mentions prominent people. Here are brief introductions and other bits of information.

I met General Gordon Bennett, the defender of Singapore, rather informally. He arrived one sleepy afternoon in a Lockheed Hudson, and I happened to be the only one around with a car. I walked up, not knowing who he was, said I was Captain Allen, Army Air Force, and did he need a ride? He did, so Bennett and I went up to the mess alone, after inspecting my live torpedo which I kept in the hangar for emergency use, he and I had a couple of drinks. I finally asked him what his name was and he said Gordon Bennett. We had another drink and I thought he was an OK guy. Pretty soon a bevy of aides, Heflin, Delaroo, etc. arrived, bowing and scraping: Lt. General Gordon took it in his stride, smiled and bought the next round. It is true: "Generals and 2ⁿᵈ Lts. are the easiest people to work with."

Lt. General Gordon Bennett (1887-1962) Australian Army – Had just landed at Perth. A tardy welcoming committee rushed in; Lt. Allen learned Bennett was reporting to take command of Army III Corps in Perth. Active in both World Wars, he distinguished himself at Gallipoli fighting with the ANZAC forces and later on the Western Front. He was "mentioned" in dispatches multiple times and awarded the DSO, Order of the Bath and other prestigious citations. Between the wars he was the most senior Army officer but was not named to command the Australian Army. He was outspoken and his escape when Singapore surrendered was controversial. He was transferred to Reserve of Officers, May 1944. Retired to the farm and died in 1962.

Vice Admiral John S. "Slew" McCain, Sr. (1864-1965) USN – Annapolis class 1906. Served on President Teddy Roosevelt's Great White Fleet around the world cruise, 1907- 1908. He was a pioneer of Aircraft Carrier Operations; received flight training at age 52. January 1941 promoted to Rear Admiral, Commander at North Island when Pearl Harbor was attacked. His personality was forthright, gruff and often "Sea-dog" profane. He enjoyed gambling and drinking. He was a natural inspirational leader. May 1942 he was named Commander Aircraft South Pacific COMAIRSOPAC – with authority over land-based Allied Air Ops supporting the Guadalcanal and Solomon Islands' campaign. He personally selected sites for navy bases in the Coral Sea area. October 1942 he was called to DC as head of Navy Bureau of Aeronautics. August 1943 appointed Vice Admiral Deputy Chief Naval Operation for Air. October 1944 Command Task Force 38. He attended the surrender ceremonies in Tokyo Bay 1945. "Slew" was slated to be Deputy Director of VA under General Omar Bradley. He was posthumously promoted to Admiral.

Lt. General George Howard Brett (1886-1963) USAAF - West Point class of 1906. Served with Philippine Scouts and 2nd Cavalry: Transferred to Aviation Signal Corps Sept. 1916. Served with Gen.

Billy Mitchell in France. Between wars served at various posts and attended Army War College. While in Panama Canal Zone his eldest daughter, Dora, married his aide, Lt. Bernard A. Schriever (Texas A&M 1931); April 1942 Commander Allied Air Forces Southwest Pacific in Melbourne. 19th Bomb Group of old B-17s; one rescued MacArthur in Mindanao, PI; another, his personal plane, "The Swoose," a B-17D, is on display at AF Museum. July 1942, MacArthur selected Gen Kenney to be theater Air Commander. Nov. 1942 he was appointed commander Caribbean Defense Command including Panama. He retired in 1945.

Lt. General George Churchill Kenney (1898-1977) USAAF - MIT – 1910, civil engineer studies and worked on railroads. In Nov. 1917 he joined the Air Service, was an aviator in France, CO of the 91st Observation Sqdn. In 1919 he was CO 8th Aero Sqdn. patrolling the Mexican border. He attended Army War College in 1932. He was involved in B-17 evaluation. In 1938 C O 97th Observation Sqdn, Mitchell Field, NY. In 1939 as Chief of Production Engineering, Wright Field, he upgraded aircraft armament from .30 caliber to .50 caliber machine guns and promoted leak-proof fuel tanks. At 4th Air Force in San Francisco he instructed pilots in the Lockheed P-38 Lightning. July 1942 he took over Supreme Commander Douglas MacArthur's 5th Air Force and received an hour-long lecture on Air Force shortcomings. Recognizing that Doug knew nothing about air operations he was patient and established a good relationship. He had technical representative, Charles Lindbergh, instruct pilots on how to extend the range of the P-38. The Southwest Pacific was low priority for replacement of aircraft so he organized and engaged at squadron level methods to protect airplanes. He adopted innovative tactics like leap-frog bombing missions and low-level skip-bombing. In June 1944 he was promoted to command Far East Air Force (FEAF) which included 5th, 13th and 7th Air Forces. He received his 4th star 9 March 1945. Post-war he briefly commanded SAC and then the Air University, retiring in 1951. He said of the strong design of the B-26, "It takes care of itself and comes home."

Brigadier General Howard Huston "Pursuit" George (1892-1942) USAAF, Enlisted Private in NY National Guard, promoted to sergeant while chasing Pancho Villa on the Mexican border in 1916. He enlisted in Aviation Section Signal Corps, 15 April 1917, commissioned pilot Lt. 15 Sept. 1917. In September 1918 he joined 139 Aero Squadron; while on patrol October 27 he struck a formation of four enemy Fokkers. On 5 November 1918 he gained his 5th victory and became an Ace. He received a Regular Army commission as Captain Air Service in 1922. In 1929 he served at France Field, Panama for two years. In 1938 he attended Command and General Staff School. Was given commanded 94th Pursuit Squadron, 1st Pursuit Group, and Selfridge Field, Michigan. 5 May 1941, now, Colonel George arrived in Manila, Philippines with Brig. Gen. Henry Clagett, 5th Interceptor Command. In mid-December Clagett went to Australia and George inherited the Pursuit Command as *de facto* commander of remaining Army aviation units. He was promoted Brig. Gen. 25 January 1942 and made his command post on Bataan Peninsula. On 11 March 1942 he was evacuated from Corregidor by PT boat along with General MacArthur. George was killed in a ground accident at Batchelor Field, Darwin, Australia when a P-40, on takeoff, lost directional control and struck a group of officers standing next to the transport plane in which they had just arrived. He is honored at George Air Force Base, Victorville, California.

Peyton M. Magruder (1911-1982) Aeronautical Engineer, He was a young man in a hurry matching the speed of his future brain-child airplane, the B-26. He received appointments to both West Point and Annapolis; chose the latter but with his head in the air, he took off in his senior year to enroll in the new Aeronautical Engineering discipline at the University of Alabama. A talented aero designer, he wished for hands-on opportunities to polish his advanced ideas. A family friend, Admiral Earnest King, Chief of the Navy's Bureau of Aeronautics, suggested he join the staff at the Naval Aircraft Factory in Philadelphia. Here they not only produced planes but also devised and tested production techniques. Moving on with this priceless résumé Glenn L. Martin grabbed him. An innovative junior engineer at age 27, his imaginative concept impressed Mr. Martin and he was appointed Project Engineer for Model 179. It won top numbers in Air Corps evaluation. They called it B-26 and ordered 201 right off the drawing board. Martin airplane nick-names always began with "M." The RAF called 179 the 'Marauder'; everyone liked it… the name stuck… the rest is history. But there's more. Peyton was instrumental in designing the Martin machine gun turret that was installed on most warplanes, not just Martin models. Also, a conversation with Col. "Jake" Harmon at Wright Field Bombardment Section led to rigging the B-26 as an Army torpedo carrier. He agreed the keel would support the heavy weapon and devised a supporting saddle. He also warned the arrangement would create drag thus diminishing the Marauder's speed advantage.

Mr. Peyton M. Magruder, B-26 designer, visiting 397th BG in England to get first-hand information on the plane's performance. Left to Rt. Lt. Col. Richard McLeod; Mr. Magruder; host: Lt. Col. Franklin Allen, and Lt. Col. Burkenkamp – all are squadron commanders in Col. Richard Coiner's 397th "Bridge Buster" Group.

Colonel Franklin S. Allen, Jr. (1918-1976) "A pilot's pilot"; University of Oregon, BS Journalism. Joined Army Air Corps pilot training class 1940-A, had a 29-year USAF career, retiring January 1968. He served with the 22nd BG 19th BS in the Southwest Pacific. He had a life-long interest in firearms and was a member of the National Rifle Association; he was a qualified *expert sharpshooter;* it was a natural match to select (then 1st Lt Allen) for special assignment to a technologies experiment testing if and how a Naval aerial torpedo and an Army B-26 could become a formidable weapons system. He researched, tested and trained torpedo launching crews; he could be called – Army Air Corps "Mr. Torpedo." Frank had a favorite gun story: An aerial gunner in the 22nd Group was credited with a "kill" after he accidentally dropped his machine gun out of the tail position and it fell on a Zero's propeller causing it to crash. Captain Allen flew 18 combat missions over New Guinea and Rabaul with the 19th BS and later, in Europe, Lt. Col. Allen, CO of the 598th Squadron, 397th BG, flew 46 combat missions and earned the DFC, (Distinguish Flying Cross), Air Medal and Presidential Unit Citation.

Lt. Col. Merrill T. Dewan (1918-1963) USAF Reserve. Known as "Jo-Jo" to his combat crew. Bachelor of Science, Syracuse University, an articulate writer we were privileged to know Merrill by his daily diary entries, beginning in Chapter 13. His son Tom shared this: Nov. 5, 1942, *Watertown NY Daily Times* – First Lt. Merrill Dewan an aviator, in Australia, has been decorated with the Army's Silver Star for outstanding bravery in action. The citation reads in part – "During a mission over heavily defended Lae, New Guinea the airplane electrical system failed....bombs wouldn't release. Merrill and the Bombardier, standing on the narrow passageway with bomb-bay doors open, triggered bomb release as they made a second pass over the target." Merrill remained active in the Air Force reserve. He was also active, since 1951, as a member of the NY State Department of Environmental Conservation. His last assignment was Superintendent of the Bureau of Forest Fire Control. Action and romance: Lt. Dewan and Lt. James Muri married their sweethearts, Elsie Howe and Alice Moyer ("Susie-Q") in a dual ceremony in Tucson AZ, December 25, 1941, during their final stateside training before going overseas.

Lt. Col. James P. Muri (1918-2013) USAF Reserve. The "barnstorming" B-26 pilot that buzzed the flight deck of an enemy carrier in the heat of battle – Midway June 4, 1942 – Was a farm-ranch boy from Cartersville, Montana. He had his eyes on the sky when, in the 1930s Ford tri-motors carried passengers out of nearby Billings, he saw them fly over the ranch. He may have seen stunt fliers at a county fair. He was determined to fly and joined the Air Corps right out of High School, became a welder and opted for pilot training. (His story details are in the Cover Story chapter.) Dogged by Zero fighters during the battle, he launched his torpedo; it didn't run true but news of his escape captured the imagination and Jim became a true Air Corp legend. During his 24-year Air Force career, he inspired young fliers and served as an Air Attaché as well as Operations Officer in various Active units. He retired in 1959 to his home in Montana.

Flying Cadet Class 40-A: Cadets entered training June 1939 – Graduated on March 23, 1940 commissioned 2nd Lt. Army Air Corps – assigned to active duty 1 May 1940. As stated in their class history: "40-A was made up of 'special' types of personalities. 94% of 219 were college graduates. Seven were college class presidents, 28 were inter-collegiate athletic captains, nine were football captains, five were rifle champions, 15 were fraternity presidents, 19 were professional society presidents, and six were editors-in-chief of their respective college publications. Two graduates advanced in rank to become four-star Air Force generals – General David A. Burchinal, (1915-1990) and another (name not found in time for this report.) This class, 40-A, was the first group of young men recruited in an expanded training program to provide more pilots for the new Air Corps. Lt. Franklin Staples Allen, Jr. BA in Journalism, University of Oregon was in this class.

Censoring Letters – People to People – To Lt. Allen's free-wheeling spirit it's a pain in the butt to know a "censor" is looking over his shoulder watching for words that are a "no-no" so with a touch of humor he pens an all purpose "Dream Letter" to satisfy the most stringent censorship rules.

Dear_____, After leaving where we were before we arrived and not knowing we were coming from there to here, we couldn't tell when we would arrive here, but never the less, we are now here and not there. The weather here is just as it is at this season, but of course quite unlike the weather where we were before we came here. After leaving by what we left by, we had a good trip, the land and water being just like it would be here and not like anything there. The people are just like they look but don't look like they do where we came from. The distance from there to here is just as far as from here to there, so there is nothing to be alarmed about. The way we came here is just the way everyone comes here from there. We had to bring everything we had with us for what we wear here is not the same that we wore there. The whole experience here is also not the same as it was there. The houses here are not like the houses where we were before coming here. The time here is the same time we had there. It is now time to end this newsy letter before I give away too much valuable information as the Censor here is liable to be a spy. (signed_____)

Appendix F

Battle of the Coral Sea

"Scratch one Flattop! Dixson to carrier, Scratch one Flattop." Lt. Commander Robert E. Dixson's (later Rear Admiral Dixson) words were piped to all-hands and "Lady Lex" erupted with cheers. A reporter on board the aircraft carrier Lexington said, "The crew exploded with cheers." Commander Dixson led SBD dive bombers from the *USS Lexington* and sunk the first Japanese aircraft carrier in World War Two – the light aircraft carrier "*Shoho.*" The Battle "that saved Australia" occurred May 4 – 8, 1942. This was the opening salvo of aircraft carrier warfare in the Pacific.

The guidelines for Japan's "Southern Advance" which began December 8, 1941 (Sunday, December 7th in Hawaii) were boldly spelled out In the Japanese Army – Navy Central Agreement of November 1941. ***"Reduction of the primary foundation of American, British and Dutch power in Eastern Asia, the occupation of the Southern Areas."*** The multi surprise "kickoffs" were well coordinated at Pearl Harbor, the Philippines, Malaysia and Netherlands East Indies. Japan's *"Kido Buti"* – Mobile Force – clearly demonstrated the mobility, range and striking power of a carrier fleet. Air cover was indispensible to protecting invasion forces as well as destroying high-seas fleets. On December 10th the British battleship *Prince of Wales* and heavy cruiser *Repulse* were spotted by land-based aircraft and promptly attacked. The ships hesitated in calling for air cover and were the first capital ships in history to be sunk solely by aircraft. Reporting this grave news to Parliament, Prime Minister Winston Churchill said: *"Over the vast expanse of waters Japan was supreme, and we everywhere were weak and naked."* So confident of their invincible power, four Fleet carriers conducted a massive raid (19 Feb.) on the port of Darwin on the Australian mainland. By February 7, 1942 after two months of fighting and advancing down the Malay Peninsula, Japanese forces besieged Singapore, "Gibraltar of the East." The city surrendered on February 15. Contrary to popular belief, the big coast artillery guns were turned inland and shelled advancing troops. Unfortunately the ammunition was armor-piercing shells intended to destroy battleships. High explosive shells were needed to effectively win land battles.

It was springtime in Japan, April, 1942. With a backdrop of beautiful cherry blossoms and spirits buoyed by sweet success in the Southern Area, the Imperial High Command debated two schools of thought, whether to continue territorial gains or to wage an all-out pursuit of American carriers in the Pacific. Admiral Yamamoto preferred the latter. Yamamoto's position had merit but adoption seemed as elusive as the American carriers. Then the unthinkable happened – April 18, 1942, – Sixteen B-25 bombers commanded by Lt. Col. James H. Doolittle, launched from the carrier *Hornet,* stunned the Japanese by bombing targets in the Home Land – the first time in centuries that Japan proper had been attacked. Needless to say, Yamamoto's plan was immediately adopted. The Army – Navy Central Agreement also stated: ***"In case of attack by strong American Force, at suitable opportunity, assemble major portion of Combined Fleet and destroy enemy."*** For Admiral

Isoroku Yamamoto, Doolittle's raid was a "strong force." He set his sights on two ambitious operations. First, occupy Port Moresby and the Solomon Islands, then mount the duel, Midway – Aleutian operations. If successful, Australia would be isolated and hopefully the American carriers would be lured into a decisive battle. His grand plan had a problem. Code breaker, Captain Joseph J. Rochefort, led the team that broke the Japanese Naval General Operational Code in March 1942; they called it JN-25b. Admiral Nimitz had the ability to intercept, decode and read enemy radio messages. With access to Japanese battle plans; he was able to outwit Yamamoto's forces. But Nimitz also had a problem – limited resources.

Vice Admiral Frank J. Fletcher's carrier fleet had only two fleet carriers, *USS Lexington* and *USS Yorktown* (128 airplanes), plus the refueling tanker (oiler) *Neosha* and a flotilla of 13 destroyers. Unfortunately the brand new carrier *Hornet* and veteran carrier *Enterprise* were returning from the Tokyo Raid so they were not available. It would take those carriers five days to replenish their stores. Also, the *USS Saratoga* was away getting a full refit at Puget Sound. Japanese Vice Admiral Takeo Takagi had Fleet carriers *Shokaku (Soaring Crane)* and *Zuikaku (Auspicious Crane)* and the light carrier *Shoho (Happy Phoenix)* – he believed they were more than a match to take-on the enemy. Meanwhile, Japanese troops had landed on the north coast of New Guinea at Lae – Salamaua and were preparing a fleet assisted landing to seize Port Moresby on the Islands' southern coast.

Both carrier forces entered the Coral Sea on May 5th and maneuvered for battle southeast of New Guinea. The battle began on May 7th and *Shoho* was sunk. Carriers *Shokaku* and *Zuikaku* were also under attack and could not provide air cover as promised for landings at Port Moresby. The American carriers were damaged as well and the oiler *Neosha* was critically damaged and adrift. It was later scuttled. Japanese Vice Admiral Inoue realized without air cover his Port Moresby landing operation would be lost. He ordered a withdrawal. This, for the record, was the first time Japan had been stopped from reaching its major objective. They did however occupy Tulagi a small island in the Solomon's near Guadalcanal.

On May 8th, the second day of battle, Lady Luck abandoned *"Lady Lex."* She was critically damaged by two, Type 91, "Long Lance" torpedoes and by internal explosions. Adrift, she was later sunk by a friendly torpedo. Destroyer *Sims* was also hit by three bombs; broke in half and sank. The *Yorktown* limped back to Pearl Harbor for quick repair and, a month later, participated in the Battle of Midway – until she was sunk. Historically the Coral Sea battle marked the first time aircraft carriers engaged each other without sighting each other. Strategically it was a win for Admiral Fletcher in that two strong Japanese Fleet aircraft carriers were damaged and unable to participate in the battle of Midway. "Where were the B-26 Marauders during this period?" you ask. The 22nd BG Marauders flew their first mission April 5, 1942. Nine B-26s attacked the Japanese stronghold at Rabaul, New Britain; thus began one of the unsung epics of the war – harassing enemy air-power and turning back an attempt to capture Port Moresby. Read more in **Chapter 12 – Battle Stations.**

Appendix G

An Engineer's War

Colonel Dwight D. Eisenhower, on General Marshall's staff in Washington D.C, in mid-December 1941, recommended that Australia be developed to support General Douglas MacArthur in the event of war in the Far East. After the attack on Pearl Harbor, Ike's plan was activated. On Christmas Eve 1941 a troopship destined for the Philippines was diverted to Brisbane. Thus, the first U. S. troops landed in Australia. The Philippine battle was lost; General MacArthur was evacuated to Australia. In July 1942, General MacArthur moved his Headquarters from Melbourne to Brisbane to be closer to the battle in Papua New Guinea. Still closer, the small port of Townsville, Queensland, Australia, (1940 Pop. 30,000) military instillations were being built, the population grew to over 100,000 (80% military). The town became the principal transshipment point for supplies and ammunition for the battles ahead. From its airport the Southwest Pacific air-war began. B-17s of the 19th Bomb Group (H) arrived 19 February 1942; three days later they bombed the Jap strong-hold city of Rabaul, New Britain, on the Solomon Sea north of the Coral Sea.

In the vicinity of Townsville a complex of airfields for fighters and medium range bombers would be built. Each airfield would be locally identified. To avoid confusion Townsville airport was renamed **Gorbutt Field**, adopting the name of a nearby subdivision built in the 1930s by the Gorbutt Brothers, wholesale meatpackers. Their facility bordering the airport had a railroad spur for cattle-cars and now would handle aircraft repair supplies. In the rural area near the town of **Woodstock** and village of **Charters Tower**, about 35 mile south of Townsville, three airfields were built. The U.S.46th EGS (Engineer General Service) moved in and started moving earth. This outfit was also a Combat Engineer Regiment and when they received an invasion alert, 3 May 1942 – work stopped – they picked up rifles and .50 caliber machine guns (they had no heavy weapons) and proceeded to an outpost overlooking Giru Railroad Junction. It was a false alarm – so back to work.

"The strips were rough and crude but airplanes could land on them." recalls Engineer CO Lt. Col. Albert G. Matthews. He said, "The first strip was named **Reid River.** The south bank of the river was favored as the camp site." In the later part of April the 18th BS operated from this strip. The 22nd BG flew their first mission from Garbutt Field on 5 April 1942. The field had been expanded and reporters said, "It was a sight to see the B-26 airplanes taxi down Duckworth Street to their new home on the north side of the runway. Crew Chiefs' had the honor of driving."

The 19th BS moved from Garbutt Field to **Woodstock** 4 July 1942 and remained there until **Iron Ridge** was ready. In early June 1942 U.S. Engineers began work in dense rainforest on the Claudie River near Lockhart River Mission – clearing away frogs, pythons, parrots and exotic birds making way for a different "exotic" bird – the B-26. This location in far North Queensland was a fall-back airfield only one-hour flight-time across the Coral Sea to Port Moresby on the south shore of New Guinea. Two unsealed strips were available and the 19th BS moved in 15 September 1942; they stayed until 4 February 1943 when they returned to **Woodstock.** Another airfield was **Antil Plains** occupied 5 July 1942 until 29 September by the 33rd BS when it too, went to **Iron Ridge**, staying until 4 February 1943 when it returned to **Woodstock.**

Other significant construction, in and around, Townsville, included medical facilities. With Nurses – who pleasantly enhanced the social scene at airfield soirées. ***Editor's note:*** *We pause here to "Construct" the most important camp building the **Officers' Club**, a do-it-your-self-project. Merrill fills us in: I worked all afternoon cleaning up the O.C. 'Wallaby Castle'… On October 6, the boys worked building the dance floor for the dance we are throwing Thursday nite for American nurses that are stationed in Townsville and Charters Tower… On October 8, the big nite – the party – about 25 nurses were present. We had a little 4-piece orchestra – not bad – quite a gala affair, with everyone lit to the ears – nurses and all… Next morning, October 9, everyone recovering – no flying.*

The 12th Station Hospital was moved from Brisbane to Townsville in March 1942. Private homes (33) were obtained along Chapman Street. Interior walls were removed and ramps were built connecting each house, on both sides of the street. Satellite Station hospitals were built – 200 bed capacity – at four locations, including **Woodstock** – (it later became) **2nd Field Hospital**, single story prefabricated huts became wards and recreation buildings. The 3rd Platoon of this hospital established a tent evacuation hospital at Milne Bay, New Guinea. The SeaBees, (Navy Construction Battalion) constructed two small (120 & 100 beds) hospitals in Townsville. As the war moved on, these facilities were deactivated and dismantled. Airfields were also abandoned. In September 1944 General MacArthur moved his HQ to New Guinea – when commenting on what it took to support one shooting soldier, he said, "Look at these facilities – all this construction – it is an *Engineer's War.*"

Appendix H

The *Flak-Bait* Story

The lifespan of a combat airplane is measured in missions flown—battle damage is quickly repaired and the plane is fit to fly another day – this carefully tallied longevity count is a worthy testament to the skill of Crew Chiefs and their supporting aircraft mechanics plus the inherent sturdy structural design of the plane. When designing the B-26, Peyton Magruder gave it a strong central keel and smooth aerodynamic lines. It was a "Hot" ship requiring skillful piloting, "pampered" maintenance and better than basic landing facilities. Rudimentary airfields quickly thrown up around Townsville, Australia and frontline strips at Port Moresby, New Guinea took their toll in wear and tear on the B-26. Meanwhile, another Medium bomber, the B-25 Mitchell, appeared in the combat theater. With a lighter wing load it got off the ground quicker after a short runway run which exposed it to fewer "potholes and pebbles" thus resulting in fewer maintenance problems. It was the "darling" of Maintenance Officers and became the preferred bird in the Southwest Pacific.

Army Air Forces' (AAF) planners shifted all B-26 Marauders to Africa and the European Theater of Operations (ETO). The Allies invaded North Africa in November 1942. B-26Bs of the new 319th Bomb Group flew their first mission on 4 December 1942. As the Allies progressed along the Mediterranean and invaded Italy, the 319th BG moved to Sardinia in October 1943. It and the 320th BG, during February 1944, bombed Abbey de Monte Cassino. The first Marauder to log 100 missions was "Hell's Bells II" with the 319th reaching that milestone in May 1944. The B-26 was racking-up an enviable record – the AAF lost fewer Marauders than any Allied bomber it flew in combat – less than one-half of one percent.

The National Air & Space Museum's B-26B nicknamed *Flak-Bait* (AAF serial number 41-31773) survived 207 operational missions over Europe, more than any other American aircraft during World War I I. Workers at the Glenn L. Martin, Baltimore, Maryland plant completed *Flak-Bait* in April 1943 and a crew flew it to England. It was assigned to the 449th Bombardment Squadron, 322th Bomb Group (nicknamed 'Annihilators'), with fuselage identification code PN-O. Lt. James J. Farrell of Greenwich, Connecticut, flew more missions in *Flak-Bait* than any other pilot. He named the bomber after "Flea Bait," his brother's nickname for the family dog.

This Marauder earned its nickname after just a few missions. Other bombers often returned unscathed but *Flak-Bait* invariably returned full of holes. "I was hit plenty of times, all the time," recalls Farrell. "I guess I was hit more than any other plane in the Group." The 100 mission mark was reached 1 June 1944, making it the third Marauder based in Britain to hit the century-mission mark. The bomber soaked up 700 metal splinters on mission 180 in March 1945. On 10 September 1943 during a mission to Amiens, France, a Messerschmitt Bf 109 approached unseen out of the sun, it attacked and a 20 mm cannon shell penetrated the Plexiglas nose, wounding the bombardier and exploding against the back of the instrument panel. Despite having his instruments knocked out, and a metal fragment lodged in his leg, Farrell brought **Flak-Bait** back to England. "It was the best landing I ever saw the boss make," commented Sgt. Don Tyler, tail gunner. During other missions, **Flak-Bait** gunners downed at least three German aircraft but only one was officially credited to the bomber. The first crew returned home, July 1944. The airplane was assigned to another crew and then reassigned to Lt. Henry "Hank" Bozarth of Shreveport, Louisiana. "Everybody was afraid of the damn thing," remembers McDonald Darnell, Jr., Bozarth's radio operator, "but she always got back for us. We always had faith in her."

"Flak-Bait's" hour of glory came 17 April 1945, when it completed its 200th mission, leading the entire 322nd BG to Magdeburg, Germany and back. During its career, this bomber flew from four airfields, two of them on the continent after D-Day. She logged 725 hours of combat time. She returned twice on one engine and once with an engine on fire, suffered complete electrical failure twice and lost the hydraulic system on one mission. She bombed coastal targets, flew two missions on D-Day, and 21 missions against V-1 (buzz bomb) launching sites in the Pas de Calais area of France, and attacked targets in the Netherlands and Belgium. The 322nd was the first American bomb group in Europe to bomb in force at night. She flew three night bombing missions.

When the war ended in Europe, General Henry H. "Hap" Arnold selected **Flak-Bait** to be included in a collection of World War II aircraft from different countries to be set aside for the National Aeronautical Collection. The Air Force transferred the bomber to the National Air Museum in May 1949. The nose portion was on display at the Smithsonian Air Museum on the Mall in Washington D.C. It was moved to the suburbs in 1960. More than a thousand patched Flak holes bear witness to the fact that this famous B-26B Marauder was appropriately named. When reassembling is complete **Flak-Bait** will be displayed proudly the same way she appeared on a forward battlefield-airfield in Europe, **May 8, 1945 . . . VE-Day.**

Bibliography

Brown, Kenneth T. *Marauder Man*. New York, NY: ibooks, Simon & Schuster, 2001

Caidin, Martin *The Ragged, Rugged Warriors,* New York, NY: E.P. Dutton, Ballantine Books, 1966

Center - Air Force History, *USAAF – WW I I Combat Chronology*, Wash. DC: Carter, Kit C. 1991

Dewan, Merrill Thomas. *Red Raider Diary*. Pittsburgh, PA: RoseDog Books, 2009

Fuchida, Mitsuo, *Midway: the Battle that Doomed Japan,* Annapolis, MD: Naval Institute, 1955

Havener, J. K. The Martin B-26 Marauder. St. Petersburg FL: Southern Heritages Press, 1968

Hickey, Lawrence J. *Revenge of the Red Raiders*. Boulder CO: Int'l Research Corp. 2006

Michener, James A. *Tales of the South Pacific*. New York: Macmillan Publishing Co., 1947

Mrozek, Donald J. *A Wartime Love Story*. Manhattan KS: Sunflower University Press, 1980

Spurrier, William Roy *World War I I Memoir.* San Francisco, CA: Blurb Press Inc., 2014

Walsh, Stan *First Over the Front.* Bloomington, IN: AuthorHouse, 2011

Index

Printed in the United States
By Bookmasters